STUDENT
THESAURUS

Elizabeth A. Ryan

Troll Associates

Illustrated by Rick O'Boyle

Introduction

How to Use Your Thesaurus

Have you ever tried to think of a word—and couldn't? No matter how hard you think, the right word just won't come to you.

Well, you're not alone. This happens to nearly everybody at times. And that's why a *thesaurus* is so helpful and handy. It can quickly give you the word you need and want.

A thesaurus is a book that gives many different suggestions for words that you can use. It lists several alternative words beside one main word. In this book, the different words printed in black are *synonyms* for the main word, printed in heavy dark type. That means that they have the same or almost the same meaning. The words listed in red are *antonyms* for the main word. That means that they have the opposite or almost the opposite meaning.

Some main words have more than one meaning (for example, "appear"). After each of these words are numbered groups of synonyms. The more meanings a main word has, the more numbered groups of synonyms it has after it.

Some main words have the same spelling but are not said the same way (for example, "close" and "close"). They are different words with different meanings. Numbers appear in front of these words. That will tell you they're different words that happen to look the same. The group of synonyms following each of these numbered words belongs to that word only.

Let's suppose you are writing a paper. After a while, you realize that you are using the word "good" too much. Look up the main word "good" in this thesaurus. You'll find several other choices for words that mean the same or nearly the same as "good." You might choose one of the words that is listed. Or you might think of still another word, on your own, just by looking at the list.

All the main words in this thesaurus are listed in alphabetical order. To help you find the main word you're looking for, a pair of *guide words* appears in dark type at the top of every page. They tell you what the first and last listings are on each page, so you can determine what main words fall between them.

For example, the guide words on page 20 are **break** and **building**. So, while you could find the main word **bright** on this page, the listings for **branch** and **by** would not be there.

Sometimes, you won't be able to find a listing for a word at all. In that case, try to think of another word close to it in meaning. Then look that second word up in the thesaurus.

If that doesn't work, check a dictionary. The definition of a word can often lead you to synonyms for it.

Keep in mind, however, that a thesaurus is not a dictionary. A dictionary tells you what a word means. A thesaurus only lists words very much alike or opposite a given word.

Many of the synonyms listed here have slightly different meanings from the main word. For example, under "youngster" is listed "youth, minor, child, kid, adolescent." Each of these is a word for a different kind of youngster:

A *youth* is a teen-ager or young person in his or her twenties.

A *minor* is anyone under legal age (18 or 21).

A *child* is thought of as between the ages of three and twelve. The word is used to identify a relationship to particular parents.

A *kid* is an informal word for "child."

An *adolescent* is a teen-ager or someone roughly between ages 10 and 20.

The thesaurus will not explain these different shades of meaning. If you aren't sure of something, look it up in your dictionary. What the thesaurus will do is give you the chance to know about some new words. It will also help you remember some old words you may have forgotten.

Whatever you do, *don't give up.* Sooner or later, you'll find a word that meets your need. And every time you do, you'll improve your ability to speak and write.

A

abandon   leave, forsake, surrender, depart, withdraw, desert

ability   talent, skill, knack, capacity, know-how, *inability*

able   skillful, capable, competent, efficient, *unable*

abnormal   irregular, odd, unnatural, peculiar, *normal*, *usual*, *average*

about   1. nearly, around, almost, approximately

about   2. regarding, concerning, respecting, of, touching

above   on, upon, overhead, *below*

abroad   overseas, away

abrupt   curt, unexpected, sudden, hasty

abrupt

absent   missing, truant, gone, away, not present, *present*

absolute   perfect, true, complete, thorough, total, *partial*

absorb   soak up, sponge, suck up, take in, incorporate, integrate

abstract   theoretical, difficult, *concrete*

absurd   ridiculous, nonsensical, unbelievable, silly, foolish, ludicrous, impossible, meaningless, *sensible*, *meaningful*

absurd

abuse   damage, mistreat, curse, insult, scold, ill-use

5

academy college, school, high school, institution

accent emphasis, stress, tone, inflection, pronunciation, voice

accept allow, take in, adopt, approve, believe, agree to, *deny*

accident chance, fluke, mishap, casualty, injury

accidental casual, chance, incidental, *deliberate, intentional*

accomplish achieve, complete, execute, carry out, do, perform, fulfill

accord agreement, harmony, treaty

account report, description, tidings, information, statement, story, reason

accumulate gather, amass, collect, grow, store up, increase, assemble, compile

accumulate

accurate exact, precise, correct, right, perfect, *inaccurate, wrong*

accuse charge, tattle, blame, denounce, indict

ache hurt, pain, agony, anguish, throb, soreness

achieve accomplish, attain, reach, fulfill, perform, carry out, succeed, complete, *fail*

act do, perform, function, behave, pretend

action deed, behavior, feat, performance

active working, energetic, lively, vivacious, dynamic, peppy, spirited, animated, agile, brisk, alert, *inactive, lazy*

act

activity movement, energy, action, occupation

actor   performer, player, entertainer, trouper

actual   real, factual, genuine, concrete, true, authentic, veritable, *nonexistent*

add   sum up, join, increase, put together, unite, total, *subtract*

additional   extra, more

address   abode, home, place

adequate   ample, enough, plenty, sufficient, satisfactory, *inadequate*, *insufficient*

adjust   arrange, alter, vary, modify, change, regulate, set

admire   like, esteem, regard, respect, appreciate

admit   1. acknowledge, confess, *deny*

admit   2. receive, induct, allow to enter, *refuse*

adopt   choose, accept, assume

adore   worship, love, idolize, cherish, admire, revere, *hate*, *despise*

adorn   decorate, ornament

adult   full-grown, developed, of age, grown-up, mature, ripe, *childish*, *immature*, *juvenile*

advance   move forward, progress, proceed, march, *recede*, *retreat*

advantage   benefit, leverage, gain, profit, superiority, *disadvantage*

adventure   exploit, experience, undertaking, hazard, enterprise, project

advertise   publicize, promote, announce

adore

7

advice counsel, recommendation, suggestion, instruction, plan, direction, tip

advise counsel, suggest, recommend, direct, instruct

affair 1. event, occasion, happening, party

affair 2. interest, business, concern

affect influence, shape, change, cause

affection regard, warmth, fondness, liking, *dislike*

afraid scared, alarmed, frightened, fearful, cowardly, timid, *unafraid, fearless, brave*

afterward later, subsequently, following

again anew, once more, repeatedly, another time

against opposed to, opposite, averse to, facing, versus, *for*

agency office, operation, bureau

agony grief, pain, suffering, anguish, distress, torture, torment

agree go along with, consent to, approve of, comply with, harmonize, *disagree, differ with*

agreement harmony, pact, contract, treaty, understanding, bargain, deal

ahead before, forward, leading, winning, onward

aid assist, help, relieve, support, serve, remedy, *hinder*

aim intention, objective, goal, target, purpose, end

air atmosphere, oxygen, ambiance

alarm scare, startle, shock, unnerve, frighten, *soothe, calm*

affection

alert watchful, attentive, wide-awake, ready, lively, *dull*

alibi excuse, story

alien stranger, foreigner

alike identical, similar, akin, same, resembling, *unlike*

alike

alive alert, vital, lively, active, *dead*

alley lane, back street, path, aisle, corridor

allow let, grant, permit

allowance portion, ration, allotment, budget

ally friend, helper, partner, supporter

almost nearly, about, not quite, approximately, practically, somewhat, well-nigh

alone isolated, sole, solitary, solo, lonely, unaccompanied, *accompanied*

aloud noisily, audibly, distinctly, loudly, *silently, inaudibly*

also besides, too, as well, in addition

almost

alternate switch, change

always ever, forever, all the time, for good, for keeps, continually, *never*

amateur nonprofessional, beginner

amaze surprise, astonish, astound, shock, bewilder

ambition aspiration, hope, desire, drive

amend fix, change, add to, improve, correct, mend

among in with, between, surrounded by, amid

amount quantity, sum, value, measure, price

amuse

annoy

amuse   entertain, tickle, delight, divert, please, interest

amusing   delightful, funny, comical, humorous, entertaining, diverting, *dull, boring*

ancestor   forebear, predecessor, forefather, foremother

anchor   1. fix, attach, fasten, secure

anchor   2. ship hook

ancient   antique, archaic, old, aged, elderly, *modern, new*

anger   wrath, fury, annoyance, irritation, ire, temper, indignation

angry   annoyed, enraged, furious, cross, irritated, bad-tempered

animal   creature, beast

announce   proclaim, report, broadcast, declare, state, notify, tell, make known

announcement   statement, declaration, proclamation

annoy   tease, vex, disturb, irritate, make angry, pester, bother, provoke, irk

answer   response, reply, retort, rejoinder, comeback, *question*

antique   old, ancient, aged, archaic, *new, modern*

anxious   uneasy, worried, fearful, restless, troubled, agitated

apart   separate, alone

apparel   garb, clothing, attire, garments, dress

apparent   obvious, evident, visible, seeming, plain, clear

appeal   beg, implore, plead, entreat, pray, ask
appear   1. look, seem
appear   2. enter, arrive, show up, approach, arise
appearance   look, expression, air, mien
appetite   hunger, craving, desire, longing
applaud   cheer, praise, hail, acclaim, clap, *denounce*
appliance   gadget, tool, machine, device, instrument, implement, utensil

applaud

apply   use, employ, avail, utilize
appoint   name, choose, assign, nominate, elect, designate
appointment   date, engagement, meeting
appreciate   respect, enjoy, value, admire, be grateful for
approach   advance, draw near, come near
appropriate   proper, suitable, fitting, becoming, *inappropriate, improper, unsuitable, unbecoming*
approval   praise, liking, acceptance
approximately   about, closely, nearly, roughly, *exactly*
architect   builder, planner, designer
area   district, region, section, territory, zone, location, space
argue   quarrel, bicker, disagree, object, squabble, *get along, agree*
arid   waterless, dry, barren, parched, *wet*
arm   fortify, empower, equip, defend, *disarm*

armor

art

armor   shield, shell, defense, protection

army   troops, military, forces, militia, legion

aroma   fragrance, odor, perfume, scent

arrange   put in order, settle, classify, adapt, fit, sort, organize, systematize

arrest   seize, stop, apprehend, capture, check, take prisoner, *release*

arrive   show up, come, reach, get to, attain, *leave, go*

art   1. drawing, painting, design, composition, sculpture, masterpiece

art   2. skill, craft, technique, knack

article   1. essay, report, story, composition

article   2. object, item, thing

artificial   manmade, substitute, phony, fake

artist   painter, designer, sculptor, creator, author, composer

ashamed   humiliated, embarrassed, guilty, mortified, *proud*

ask   inquire, find out, request, invite, demand, *answer*

assassinate   slay, murder, kill

assault   offense, attack, onslaught, charge

assemble   1. come together, gather together, congregate, *scatter*

assemble   2. set up, build, put together, construct

assign   order, command, allot, delegate, choose, elect

assignment   chore, task, duty, portion, job, obligation

assist   support, lend a hand, help, aid, *hinder*

assistant   helper, supporter, underling, aide

assorted   mixed, various, different, several, diverse

astonishing   amazing, surprising, shocking, astounding

athletic   active, sporting, strong, muscular, brawny, gymnastic

attach   join, fasten, connect, add, affix, put together, unite, *detach*

attack   raid, siege, bombardment, assault, offense, charge

attempt   endeavor, try, undertake, make an effort, strive

attend   accompany, go to, be present, visit, *be absent*

attendant   helper, servant

attention   thoughtfulness, care, politeness, concern, consideration, courtesy

attitude   viewpoint, opinion, belief

attract   draw, pull, lure, interest, fascinate, tempt, *repel*

attractive   pretty, handsome, pleasing, winning, charming, desirable, lovely, *unattractive, plain*

attractive

audience   viewers, watchers, spectators, listeners, readers

author   writer, originator, inventor, creator

authority   command, power, influence

autograph   signature, endorsement

automobile car, vehicle, conveyance
autumn fall
available ready, handy
avenue street, boulevard, lane, road
average common, ordinary, usual, passable, fair, *extraordinary, unusual*
avoid evade, shun, dodge, avert, escape, snub
awake alert, conscious, lively, sharp, attentive
award honor, prize, reward, trophy, medal
aware conscious, informed, mindful, knowing
awe wonder, respect, fear, alarm
awful unpleasant, terrible, horrible, dreadful, vile, atrocious, *pleasant*
awkward gawky, clumsy, cumbersome, ungainly, ungraceful, unskilled, *graceful*

B

baby

babble baby talk, chatter, prattle, gabble, foolish talk
baby infant, tot, toddler, child
backward slow, behind, dull, sluggish
bad evil, wrong, naughty, unfavorable, *good*
baggage suitcases, valises, burdens, parcels

bait   tempt, lure, snare, entice, trap
balance   stabilize, steady, equalize, weigh, measure
bald   hairless, unadorned, bare, simple, open,
   uncovered, undisguised, *hairy, covered*
ballot   vote, choice, poll
band   group, orchestra, ensemble
bandage   sling, dressing, tourniquet
bandit   highwayman, robber, thief, gangster,
   brigand, outlaw
bang   strike, slam, hit, explode, clash, crash
bar   1. block, forbid, obstruct, shut out, exclude,
   prohibit, ban, *allow*
bar   2. tavern, saloon, counter
bare   naked, uncovered, nude, bald, open, *covered*
barely   hardly, scarcely, just
bargain   deal, contract, swap, trade
barrier   obstruction, barricade, bar, obstacle, wall
barter   swap, trade, exchange, deal
base   foundation, bottom
bashful   timid, shy, coy, modest
basic   fundamental, elementary, essential, underlying,
   superficial
bat   club, strike, knock, crack, hit, clobber
batch   set, bunch, group
bath   shower, washing, drenching
battle   combat, struggle, warfare, fight, conflict,
   feud, contest

bait

battle

bawl

beautiful

bawl   weep, sob, cry, howl, shout, wail

bay   harbor, inlet

beach   coast, shore, waterfront, seaside

beam   glow, smile, shine

beast   brute, animal, creature

beat   1. hit, thrash, strike, pound, pummel, knock, crack

beat   2. better, outdo, surpass, win, best, conquer

beautiful   lovely, pretty, attractive, handsome, gorgeous, *ugly*

become   develop, turn into, evolve

before   prior, earlier, formerly, previously, in advance, ahead, *after*

beg   ask, beseech, appeal, plead, implore, entreat

begin   start, launch, take off, commence, originate, initiate, *end, finish, conclude*

beginner   novice, newcomer

behave   act, mind, obey

behavior   action, manner, bearing

behind   in back of, after, later than, following, *before, ahead*

belief   credo, principle, opinion, idea

believe   1. suppose, think, imagine, consider, surmise

believe   2. trust, accept, agree with, *doubt*

belly   stomach, underside, paunch, abdomen

below   under, beneath, less, unworthy

beneath   below, under, less, unworthy, *above*

beneficial   useful, advantageous, helpful, favorable, profitable, *harmful*

bent   crooked, curved, twisted, misshapen

besides   moreover, too, also, as well, in addition

best   prime, choice, top, select, *worst*

bet   gamble, wager

between   amid, among

beyond   past, farther, exceeding

big   1. huge, tremendous, large, immense, enormous, considerable, gigantic, *small*, *little*

big   2. great, grand, important, significant, *unimportant*

big

big   3. grown-up, adult, mature, *small*, *little*

bill   charge, account, reckoning

birth   origin, beginning, infancy, inception, *end*, *death*

bite   nip, pierce, chew

bitter   unpleasant, distasteful, *sweet*, *pleasant*

blade   cutter, edge, knife, sword

blame   charge, indict, accuse, tattle, denounce, *absolve*, *forgive*

blank   vacant, empty, void

blanket   covering, coverlet, quilt

blast   blowout, explosion, burst, discharge

blaze   fire, flame, flare

bleak   discouraging, dismal, dreary, bare, chilly, cold, depressing, *cheerful*

bleed   leak, drip, drain

17

blob

bloom

blend   combine, mix, join, stir, *separate*
bless   thank, praise, hallow, glorify, *curse*
blind   eyeless, sightless, unseeing, unaware
blizzard   storm, gale, snowstorm
blob   lump, bulge, bubble
block   check, hinder, obstruct, restrain, clog, bar, stop, prevent, *permit*
blockade   obstruction, barrier, barricade, fortification
bloom   flower, flourish, grow, thrive, glow
blot   spot, mark, stain
blow   blast, puff, breeze
bluff   trick, deceive, delude
blur   dim, smear, cloud
blush   redden
board   get on, mount, embark, *get off*, *dismount*
boast   brag, preen, crow
body   carcass, corpse
boil   1. rage, seethe, fume
boil   2. bubble, simmer, cook
boisterous   rowdy, noisy, violent, rough, tumultuous
bold   1. courageous, fearless, brave, gallant, heroic, vigorous, free, clear, *cowardly*
bold   2. brazen, arrogant, defiant, insolent, *timid*
bolt   1. flee, break away, run, take flight
bolt   2. fastener, lock
bond   1. word, agreement, link, tie
bond   2. stock

boom   1. progress, gain, thrive, flourish

boom   2. explode, thunder, rumble

border   edge, margin, boundary

boring   uninteresting, dull, deadly, tiring, *interesting*

boss   1. oversee, supervise, direct, run, take charge

boss   2. supervisor, manager, employer, foreman, forewoman

boss

bother   disturb, annoy, harass, irritate, provoke, pester, worry, fuss, trouble

bottom   foundation, lowest part, base, fundament, *top*

bounce   leap, spring, jump, rebound, hop

bound   surrounded, enclosed, limited

boundary   border, limit, division, barrier

box   1. spar, hit, fight, punch

box   2. container, bin, carton, crate, case

brace   support, prop, encourage, strengthen, tighten

brag   gloat, boast, crow, flaunt, swagger

brake   slow down, stop, curb, decelerate, *accelerate*

branch   bough, limb, shoot

brand   type, sort, kind, stamp

brave   fearless, courageous, gallant, heroic, bold, valiant, unafraid, *cowardly*

brawl   quarrel, riot, racket, fracas, fight

break   1. crack, split, fracture, smash, shatter, crush, rupture, *fix, mend*

break 2. intermission, interruption, pause, recess, time out, rest, change, relaxation

breast chest, bosom

breed raise, train, produce, cultivate

bridge link, connection

brief concise, short, curt, terse, *long*

bright 1. shiny, sparkling, cheerful, vivid, gleaming, glowing, sunny, clear, *dull*, *dim*

bright 2. alert, intelligent, smart, aware, quick, lively, *dull*, *slow*

brilliant smart, wise, intelligent, clever, gifted, *stupid*

bring take, carry, deliver, transport, get

broad expansive, wide, roomy, large, *narrow*

broken burst, ruptured, shattered, imperfect

brook stream, river, creek, rivulet

bruise injure, wound, hurt, mark, mar, damage, *heal*, *soothe*

brush clean, wipe, remove, groom, rub

brutal barbaric, cruel, savage, ferocious, ruthless, mean

buddy pal, companion, chum, partner, friend, comrade

bug insect

build construct, make, establish, form, create, erect, *demolish*

building structure

bug

bulky   thick, lumpy, awkward, broad

bulletin   newsletter, message, flash, statement, announcement

bump   lump, wad, bulge, mass

bumpy   rocky, uneven, coarse, *smooth*

bunch   group, band, set, cluster

bundle   package, parcel, packet, pack

bunny   rabbit, hare

burglar   robber, thief, housebreaker

burning   sizzling, hot, fiery, blazing, flaming, flaring, scorching, charring

burst   break, explode, shatter

bury   cover, hide, conceal, entomb

business   occupation, profession, job, work, trade, affair

bustle   fuss, flurry, activity, to-do, excitement, hubbub, stir, rush

busy   engaged, active, occupied, working, *inactive*, *idle*

button   clasp, hook, fasten, close, *unbutton*, *open*

buy   shop, acquire, purchase, market, *sell*

by   beside, near, at

bumpy

busy

21

C

cab   taxi, carriage, coach, car
cabin   house, cottage, bungalow, hut
cabinet   case, cupboard, closet
cable   1. wire, telegraph
cable   2. rope, cord, wire, hawser
cafeteria   snack bar, restaurant, café, diner
cage   prison, container, enclosure
calculate   figure, compute, count, estimate, reckon

call

call   1. yell, shout, cry
call   2. telephone, summon
calm   quiet, peaceful, still, tranquil, serene, restful
camouflage   mask, disguise, fake, masquerade
campaign   movement, cause, crusade, drive
can   tin, container, receptacle
canal   waterway, aqueduct, gully
cancel   wipe out, erase, repeal, obliterate
candidate   nominee, applicant, office seeker
cap   cover, crown, top, lid
capable   able, efficient, effective, powerful, fit, competent

capture   arrest, seize, trap, catch, apprehend, grab, *release*, *free*

calm

car   automobile, sedan, vehicle
care   1. concern, thought, attention, worry

care   2. supervision, keeping, protection, custody, charge

career   calling, job, profession, occupation, trade

careful   watchful, prudent, cautious, *careless*

careless   reckless, thoughtless, sloppy, unthinking, *careful*

caress   stroke, touch, pet, fondle

carnival   festival, fair, jamboree

carpet   mat, rug, covering

carry   transport, tote, hold, take, convey

carton   case, box, container, package

carve   slice, cut, whittle

case   1. condition, circumstance

case   2. box, carton, container, package

case   3. lawsuit

cash   money, currency, coin

cast   hurl, fling, pitch, toss, throw

castle   palace, chateau, fortress, mansion

casual   informal, accidental, occasional, unexpected, *formal, planned*

catalog   classify, list, sort, group, arrange

catastrophe   calamity, misfortune, disaster, tragedy, accident

catch   seize, trap, capture, apprehend, arrest, *release*

cause   reason, origin, source, *effect, result*

cautious   careful, thoughtful, watchful, guarded, prudent

cautious

celebrate

champion

cease quit, stop, conclude, discontinue, halt, *continue*

celebrate 1. observe, commemorate, proclaim, acknowledge

celebrate 2. revel, enjoy, rejoice

cemetery burial ground, graveyard

center heart, middle, core, hub, nucleus, *fringe*, *edge*

central main, leading, principal, chief

ceremony ritual, rite, formality

certain sure, definite, positive, assured, *uncertain*

chain bind, shackle, restrain, fasten, fetter, manacle

chair bench, seat, stool

challenge defy, confront, dare, question, dispute, doubt

champion victor, winner, conqueror, best

chance 1. occasion, opportunity, opening

chance 2. likelihood, possibility, prospect

chance 3. luck, fate, fortune

change vary, alter, modify, switch, replace, substitute, *maintain*

chapter part, section, division

char burn, scorch, sear, singe

character 1. temperament, nature, disposition, makeup, personality

character 2. part, role, personage

charge attack, assault, rush, *retreat*, *flee*

charming disarming, delightful, appealing, endearing, pleasing, enchanting, alluring, *obnoxious*

chart map, plan, blueprint

chase 1. run after, follow, pursue

chase 2. reject, drive away, repulse

chat gossip, talk, converse, discuss, prattle, chatter

cheap low-priced, inexpensive, low-cost, inferior, *expensive, costly*

cheat swindle, deceive, trick, dupe, defraud, bamboozle, mislead, beguile

check 1. stop, curb, restrain, control, obstruct, hinder

check 2. verify, mark, prove

cheerful jolly, happy, gay, merry, joyful, glad, *sad, downcast*

chest locker, safe, box, dresser

chew bite, nibble, munch, crunch, grind

child baby, tot, youngster, kid, youth, offspring, *grownup, adult*

chilly nippy, bleak, cool, brisk, *warm*

chisel carve, sculpt, make

choke strangle, smother, suffocate, cough, muffle

choose select, pick, elect, opt, decide

chop sever, hack, cut, cleave, slice

chore job, task, work, assignment, duty

chorus choir, group

chubby fat, plump, stocky, stout, tubby, pudgy, fleshy, round, chunky, *skinny*

chilly

chuckle   laugh, chortle, giggle, titter, snicker

chum   pal, buddy, friend, companion, partner, comrade

chunk   lump, wad, mass, bulk

church   temple, chapel, cathedral, meetinghouse

citizen   resident, inhabitant, occupant

city   town, municipality, metropolis, urban area

claim   demand, require, insist on

clamor   ruckus, racket, uproar, commotion, din, row, hubbub, *stillness*, *quiet*

clap   applaud, knock, strike, bang

clean   stainless, spotless, unmarked, spick-and-span, clear, *dirty*

clear   1. eliminate, rid, remove, get rid of

clear   2. shining, bright, vivid, *dull*, *muddy*

clever   skillful, cunning, smart, bright, quick-witted, sharp, alert, intelligent

clever

client   patron, customer, buyer

climate   weather, temperature, environmental conditions

climb   rise, mount, ascend, *descend*

clip   1. snip, cut, shear, crop, trim

clip   2. attach, fasten

1. close   1. fasten, shut, lock, *open*

  close   2. finish, complete, end, conclude, stop, terminate, *start*

2. close   near, nearby, approaching, *far*

cloudy   overcast, dark, murky, dismal, unclear, gloomy, *clear*

club   1. association, organization, group, clique, society

club   2. stick, bat

club   3. hit, strike, knock, beat, clobber

clue   suggestion, lead, hint, evidence, sign

clump   cluster, lump, bunch

clumsy   awkward, cumbersome, ungainly, ungraceful, gawky, *graceful*

coach   teach, train, encourage, tutor

coarse   1. ragged, rocky, rough, uneven, bumpy, unfinished, *smooth*

coarse   2. vulgar, common, crude, rude, unrefined, *refined*

coax

coax   persuade, beg, plead, influence, push

code   rules, laws, arrangement, system, signal

cold   frosty, chilly, frigid, *hot*

collapse   topple, fall, break down, fail

collect   accumulate, assemble, gather, store up, *scatter*

collision   conflict, clash

colorful   vivid, bright, varied, picturesque

colossal   vast, huge, immense, enormous, gigantic, mammoth, giant, *tiny, insignificant*

combat   battle, oppose, resist, fight, struggle, contest

colossal

combine unite, blend, join, merge, mix, connect, *separate*

comedian humorist, comic

comfort 1. ease, relief, rest, enjoyment, *discomfort*

comfort 2. console, soothe, gladden, relieve, ease, assure

comfortable contented, cozy, satisfied, snug, pleasant, *uncomfortable*, *ill-at-ease*

YOU DANCE DIVINELY!

comical

comical funny, amusing, humorous, entertaining, witty, *tragic*

command order, instruct, direct, manage, control, decree

comment remark, note, observe, mention

committee council, group, delegation, commission, board

common 1. usual, regular, familiar, everyday, ordinary, expected, *uncommon*, *odd*, *unusual*

common 2. crude, vulgar, coarse, low, *refined*

commotion confusion, rumpus, action, fuss, trouble, excitement, hubbub, to-do, racket, ruckus, disturbance, *calmness*, *order*

communicate tell, pass on, inform, relay, enlighten

community neighborhood, district, town, area

companion buddy, pal, friend, comrade, chum, associate, partner

company 1. firm, business, enterprise

company 2. visitors, guests, companions

compare   liken, contrast, match, measure

competition   contest, rivalry, tournament

complain   grumble, protest, object, fret

complete   1. finish, end, wind up, conclude, close up, terminate, *start*, *begin*

complete   2. entire, whole, thorough, *incomplete*

complicated   difficult, involved, hard, complex, mixed up, *simple*

compliment   flatter, praise, congratulate, commend, applaud

conceal

compose   write, make up, create, invent

conceal   cover, hide, mask, camouflage, cloak, veil, *reveal*, *disclose*

conceited   boastful, cocky, vain, egotistical, proud, *modest*

concentrate   focus, intensify, strengthen

concern   1. worry, interest, care, trouble

concern   2. firm, company, business, enterprise

concert   recital, musical performance

conclude   finish, complete, end, close, stop, terminate, *open*, *begin*

concentrate

concrete   real, solid, actual, visible, *abstract*

condense   compress, abridge, shorten, concentrate, squeeze, reduce

condition   situation, circumstance, state, case, predicament, plight

29

confident

confuse

1. conduct   direct, manage, guide, lead

2. conduct   behavior, bearing, action, manner

confess   admit, acknowledge, concede

confident   sure, certain, positive, convinced, self-reliant, assured, *doubtful, unsure*

confuse   bewilder, complicate, baffle, muddle, perplex, puzzle, dumbfound, jumble, mistake, mix up, *clarify*

congratulate   praise, compliment, commend, acknowledge

connect   link, tie, join, unite, combine, attach, *disconnect, separate*

conquer   overthrow, overcome, defeat, overwhelm, crush, overtake, vanquish, win, triumph

consent   approval, acceptance, permission, accord, agreement, *refusal*

consequence   result, effect, outcome

conserve   save, keep, preserve, hoard, guard, maintain, *waste*

consider   ponder, think, study, imagine, contemplate, deliberate

considerate   kind, thoughtful, sympathetic, tactful, mindful, sensitive, *inconsiderate, thoughtless*

console   soothe, comfort, reassure, cheer, solace, sympathize

constantly   always, continually, unfailingly

construct   build, make, form, create, manufacture, assemble, erect, *demolish*

consult   confer, deliberate, discuss

consume   devour, eat, use up, burn up

contact   touch, connect, reach, join, approach

contain   include, hold, comprise, consist of, involve, *exclude*

contented   happy, serene, satisfied, pleased, glad, easygoing, *discontented*

contented

contest   competition, game, battle, tournament, sport

continual   enduring, incessant, perpetual, lasting

continue   keep on, go on, persist, last, endure, *stop*, *discontinue*

1. contract   deal, treaty, bargain, alliance, pact, understanding

2. contract   shrink, reduce, diminish, shorten, lessen

contribution   donation, offering, participation

control   check, curb, restrain, contain

convenient   handy, easy, suitable, nearby, *inconvenient*

conversation   discussion, dialogue, talk, chat, gossip

convert   convince, change, retool, transform

convict   sentence, condemn, doom, *acquit*, *clear*

convince   persuade, assure, make certain, reach

cool   1. frosty, chilly, cold, brisk, *warm*

cool   2. unexcited, calm, unfriendly, uninterested, *excited*

cooperate work together, support, help, collaborate, unite, *hinder*

copy reproduce, duplicate, imitate, echo, repeat

correct 1. true, right, exact, proper, accurate, appropriate, *incorrect, wrong*

correct 2. fix, improve, remedy, change, adjust

correspond communicate with, write

corridor aisle, hallway, passageway

cost price, charge, rate, expense, amount

counterfeit sham, fake, copied, imitation, artificial, *authentic, real*

country land, nation, principality, state, homeland

countryside landscape, territory, scenery

courageous gallant, bold, brave, fearless, heroic, unafraid, *cowardly*

courteous

course track, line, way, direction, channel

court 1. pursue, woo, flatter

court 2. tribunal

courteous gracious, considerate, polite, civil, respectful, obliging, *impolite, rude*

cover 1. conceal, hide, protect, shelter, *uncover, reveal*

cover 2. contain, comprise, include, consist of, involve, *exclude*

cowardly fearful, weak, timid, *courageous, brave*

coy shy, timid, bashful, modest, flirtatious, demure, *straightforward, bold*

cowardly

cozy

cozy   snug, warm, homey, comfortable

crack   split, break, open, slit, fracture

crammed   heaping, overflowing, stuffed, full, loaded, crowded, jammed, packed, gorged

cranky   irritable, cross, grouchy, disagreeable, annoyed, grumpy, bad-tempered, *good-humored*

crawl   creep, slink

crazy   mad, lunatic, insane, *sane*

crease   fold, pleat, wrinkle, furrow

create   invent, make, originate, form, produce, design, manufacture, shape, establish, cause, *destroy*

create

creative   innovative, imaginative, unusual, original

creek   river, stream, rivulet

creep   crawl, slink

crew   staff, force, team, gang, band

crime   offense, wrongdoing, law-breaking, sin, vice, evil, transgression

cringe   cower, shrink

criticize   scold, judge, censure, appraise

crook   thief, criminal, robber, gangster, lawbreaker

crop   harvest, growth, yield, result

cross   grouchy, grumpy, irritable, cranky, annoyed, disagreeable, bad-tempered, *good-humored*

crowd   throng, horde, mob, mass, group

cruel   unkind, heartless, mean, brutal, ruthless, savage, *kind*

curious

crush   squash, mash, press, compress, squeeze

cry   sob, bawl, wail, weep, howl, yowl, *laugh*

cuddle   nestle, snuggle, hug, caress

cure   remedy, heal, restore, repair, fix

curious   nosy, prying, inquisitive, snoopy, *uninterested*

current   1. existing, up-to-date, new, present, prevalent, modern, contemporary, *old-fashioned*

current   2. stream, flow, course, tide

curse   denounce, swear, condemn

curve   wind, twist, bend, curl, turn

custom   tradition, manner, habit, practice, use

customer   buyer, client, patron

cut   1. slice, dissect, snip, slit, slash, saw, sever, chop, trim

cut   2. curtail, shorten, abbreviate, condense, abridge, reduce, lessen, *lengthen, increase*

cute   pretty, charming, attractive, delightful, funny, sweet, dainty

cute

D

dainty   cute, delicate, fresh, small, pretty, fine, *gross*

damage   hurt, impair, harm, spoil, ruin, upset, *mend, fix, heal*

damp   wet, moist, humid, dank, *dry*

dangerous   hazardous, unsafe, risky, perilous, *safe*

daring   fearless, brave, heroic, courageous, bold, foolhardy, adventurous, *cautious, timid*

dark   gloomy, dreary, obscure, black, dim, dismal, somber, *bright*

darling   beloved, cherished, dear, precious, adored

daring

dart   rush, scurry, dash, hurry, scoot, *dawdle*

dash   dart, scurry, hurry, rush, scoot, *dawdle*

data   information, facts, statistics, figures, numbers

date   engagement, appointment, commitment

dawdle   linger, idle, loiter, tarry, delay, dilly-dally, *hurry*

dawn   sunrise, daybreak, *dusk*

daze   confuse, dazzle, blind, bewilder, muddle

dazzling   blinding, brilliant, glowing, sparkling, shining, glaring, glistening, shimmering, *dull*

dead   deceased, lifeless, gone, inactive, extinct, *alive*

deal   bargain, transaction, agreement, understanding, compact

dear   precious, beloved, cherished, adored

death   decease, extinction, demise

debate   dispute, argue, disagree, differ

debt   loan, obligation

decay   rot, disintegrate, spoil, crumble

deceive

decorate

deceive mislead, trick, swindle, cheat, defraud, dupe, hoax, betray

decent acceptable, proper, suitable, moral, correct, clean, respectable, right, *indecent, improper*

decide determine, resolve, judge, settle, conclude, choose

declare state, exclaim, say, announce, assert, pronounce, affirm

decorate adorn, trim, beautify, ornament

decrease lessen, reduce, diminish, shorten, cut, compress, curtail, *increase*

dedication devotion, commitment

deduct subtract, take away, remove, withdraw, *add*

deed act, action, performance

deep profound, bottomless, immeasurable

defeat outdo, surpass, win, overcome, triumph, conquer

defect flaw, fault, failing, weakness

defend safeguard, shield, protect, support, guard, *attack*

define explain, clarify, describe, interpret

definite certain, plain, obvious, clear, precise, exact, evident, clear-cut, *indefinite, unclear*

definition explanation, interpretation, meaning

deform disfigure, spoil, mar, ruin, *improve, beautify*

defy   challenge, resist, confront, disregard, disobey, flout

delay   put off, postpone, detain, stall, hold up, procrastinate

deliberately   on purpose, intentionally, purposely, knowingly, *accidentally*

delicate   fine, dainty, mild, soft, frail, light, fragile, sensitive, tender, *gross*

delicious   tasty, appetizing, savory, luscious, *tasteless*

delighted   overjoyed, elated, happy, jubilant, joyful, *unhappy*

delightful   wonderful, pleasant, lovely, charming, appealing, pleasing, *unpleasant*

deliver   convey, hand over, give, transfer, pass

delivery   transfer, conveyance, relay

delicious

demand   request, ask, insist, inquire, require

demolish   destroy, dismantle, tear apart, wreck, shatter, *restore*

demon   fiend, devil, ogre, monster, evil spirit

demonstrate   exhibit, display, show, present, illustrate, establish, prove

dense   1. crowded, compact, thick, heavy, solid, compressed

dense   2. slow, dull, stupid

dent   indent, notch, nick, depression

deny   dispute, contradict, refuse, refute, disagree, challenge, renounce

depart   withdraw, retreat, leave, go away, exit, *arrive*

dependable   reliable, trustworthy, *undependable*

deposit   put, place, leave, hoard, store, *withdraw*

depressed   disheartened, discouraged, dejected, sad, downhearted, blue, *happy*

deprived   lacking, missing, without, wanting, needing, denied

describe   depict, define, characterize, portray, tell, interpret

desert   abandon, forsake, leave, quit

deserve   be worthy of, earn, merit

design   plan, draw, sketch, paint, picture, portray

desire   want, wish, yearn, long for, crave

desperate   reckless, hopeless, despondent, frantic

despise   detest, hate, loathe, scorn, *love*, *respect*

destination   end, objective, goal

destiny   fate, fortune, lot

destroy   ruin, wreck, spoil, devastate, *restore*, *create*

detach   unfasten, separate, disconnect, untie, unhook, *join*, *attach*

detail   part, piece, portion, fraction, fragment

detective   sleuth, investigator, bloodhound

determined   firm, sure, resolute, resolved

detest   abhor, despise, hate, loathe, scorn, *love*

detour   by-pass, shift

determined

develop ripen, progress, grow, mature, flourish, advance

development growth, progress, blooming, maturation

devil fiend, monster, demon, ogre, evil spirit

devotion 1. affection, love, liking, fondness

devotion 2. dedication, loyalty, commitment, *infidelity*

devour consume, eat, swallow, use up

diagram design, sketch, drawing, blueprint

diary journal, account, record, memo book

die decease, pass away, expire, perish, *live*

different dissimilar, unlike, distinct, opposite, contrary, reverse, varied, assorted, *same, alike*

different

difficult complicated, hard, troublesome, rough, rugged, arduous, *easy*

difficulty trouble, problem, hardship, obstacle

dig excavate, scoop, tunnel, gouge

dignified stately, noble, worthy, majestic, grand, distinguished, *undignified*

dim dark, faint, dull, indistinct, cloudy, weak, vague

dimension proportions, size, measurement, expanse

dingy grimy, dirty, dark, dull, gray, *bright*

dip dunk, sink, ladle, immerse, douse

dignified

direct 1. point out, guide, lead, show, steer, escort, aim

direct 2. control, conduct, manage, lead, head, guide, dictate, order, instruct, command

director controller, leader, manager, chief, guide, superintendent

dirt grime, earth, muck, soil, filth

dirty untidy, messy, soiled, filthy, sloppy, *clean*

disadvantage handicap, drawback, inconvenience, liability, *advantage*

disagree dispute, differ, argue, oppose, quarrel, dispute, *agree*

disappear

disappear fade away, vanish, go away, evaporate, *appear, remain*

disappoint dissatisfy, frustrate, fail, displease, let down

disaster calamity, catastrophe, tragedy, misfortune, mishap, accident

disbelief skepticism, doubt, distrust, scorn, *faith, belief*

discard reject, scrap, throw away, get rid of, dispose of, *keep*

discharge release, expel, dismiss, dump, fire, let go, unload

discipline 1. train, drill, practice, prepare, condition

discipline 2. correct, punish, chastise, penalize

discomfort nuisance, handicap, trial, pest, distress, bother

discount deduction, bargain, allowance

discouraged   downhearted, dejected, depressed, disheartened, *encouraged*

discover   uncover, find, reveal, learn, notice, perceive, unearth

discover

discuss   talk over, debate, reason, consider, confer

disease   ailment, malady, infirmity, sickness, illness, *health*

disgrace   dishonor, discredit, shame, embarrassment, *honor*

disguise   mask, conceal, cover, misrepresent, camouflage, *reveal*

disgusted   revolted, sickened, nauseated, offended, repelled

dishonest   deceitful, lying, untruthful, untrustworthy, crooked, corrupt, fraudulent, *honest*

dislike   hate, loathe, disfavor, disapprove

dismal   bleak, depressing, dark, gloomy, dreary, cheerless, dull, *bright*

dismiss   expel, discharge, release, send away, brush off

disobey   defy, disregard, ignore, *obey*

display   exhibit, show, demonstrate, present, flaunt, *conceal*

display

dispute   quarrel, disagree, argue, fight, oppose, resist, *agree*

distant   far, faraway, remote, *close*, *near*

distinct

distinct   precise, exact, plain, clear, obvious, clear-cut, definite, unmistakable, *unclear*, *blurry*

distinguished   dignified, celebrated, famous, honored, outstanding, well-known, noted, popular

distract   divert, confuse, sidetrack, disturb, bewilder

distribute   allot, disperse, dispense, hand out, *collect*

district   region, area, neighborhood, section, zone, territory

disturb   annoy, upset, bother, irritate

divide   split, separate, partition, *unite*

divine   heavenly, sacred, holy, wonderful, superb

divorce   divide, separate, split, disconnect, *marry*

dizzy   confused, spinning, unsteady, giddy, staggering, *steady*

dizzy

dock   moor, anchor, tie

doctor   physician, surgeon, healer, medic

document   statement, certificate, paper

dodge   evade, avoid, elude, duck

donate   give, present, grant, bestow, contribute

done   finished, over, complete, ended, terminated, *unfinished*

donkey   ass, mule, burro

doom   destiny, fate, death

dose   amount, quantity, portion

doubt   disbelieve, mistrust, question, suspect, dispute, *believe*

downfall   failure, ruin, defeat, upset, overthrow, *success*

downpour   cloudburst, rainstorm, flood

doze   nap, sleep, drop off, drowse

drab   flat, unattractive, dull, dowdy, lifeless, *bright*

draft   1. air current, wind

draft   2. recruitment, induction, enlistment, enrollment, call-up

drag   tow, heave, pull, tug, haul, draw

drain   draw off, empty, extract, remove, dry, *fill*

drama   theater, excitement

dramatize   exaggerate, produce, present, stage, feature

draw   1. picture, sketch, design, portray

draw   2. entice, interest, attract, lure, *repel*

dreadful   wretched, awful, horrible, ghastly, terrible, unpleasant, vile, *wonderful*

dream   fantasize, imagine, muse, envision

dreary   dismal, dim, dark, gloomy, dull, somber, depressing, disheartening, *pleasant*

drench   wet, soak, saturate, immerse, flood, dunk

dress   outfit, attire, clothe, adorn, decorate

drift   wander, stray, meander, ramble, float, cruise, glide

drill   exercise, train, practice, teach, prepare, condition, discipline

dream

drink   swallow, gulp, sip, guzzle
drive   handle, steer, operate, conduct, manage
drizzle   sprinkle, shower, rain
droop   drag, sag, slump, hang, dangle
drop   fall, dive, plunge, plummet
drowsy   dreamy, sleepy, heavy-eyed, *alert*
drug   narcotic, cure, medicine, potion
drunk   tipsy, inebriated, intoxicated, besotted
dry   waterless, arid, parched, *wet*
duck   evade, dodge, sidestep, avoid, elude
dull   1. dark, dim, gray, dingy, lifeless, dreary, *bright*

dry

dull   2. dim-witted, dumb, stupid, slow, dense, *clever*, *smart*
dull   3. monotonous, boring, uninteresting, flat, dreary, *interesting*, *exciting*
dumb   1. dim-witted, stupid, dense, dull, *smart*
dumb   2. mute, voiceless, speechless, silent
dummy   1. copy, model, figure, doll, fake, mannequin
dummy   2. dope, dunce, fool
dump   throw away, empty, unload, discharge, discard, rid, *load*
dunce   dullard, simpleton, dope, dolt, fool, dummy, blockhead
duplicate   repeat, copy, double, imitate
dusk   sundown, sunset, evening, nightfall, gloaming, *dawn*

duty   chore, work, task, job, assignment, obligation, responsibility, function

dye   tint, color, stain, tinge

dying   fading, failing, sinking

dynamic   forceful, strong, active, energetic, lively, intense, spirited

E

Earth

eager   wanting, wishing, anxious, enthusiastic, ready

early   soon, recent, first, premature, *late*

earn   gain, merit, deserve, obtain, secure

earth   1. dirt, soil, sod, land, ground

Earth   2. globe, planet, world

ease   rest, repose, comfort, *difficulty*

easy   effortless, uncomplicated, simple, plain, *hard*

eat   consume, dine, chew, swallow

echo   resound, reverberate, reflect, bounce back, repeat, duplicate, imitate

eclipse   veil, blackout, shadow, cover

edge   margin, border, rim, frame

edit   revise, rewrite, correct, alter, amend, check

echo

45

eerie

educate   instruct, teach, enlighten, train, tutor, school, guide

education   schooling, learning, knowledge, training, instruction

eerie   ghostly, spooky, weird, strange, ghastly

effect   result, outcome, consequence

effective   efficient, capable, powerful

efficient   clever, useful, skillful, competent

effort   attempt, endeavor, try, undertaking, striving

elaborate   dwell on, develop, work on, detail, ornament

elastic   stretchable, flexible, springy, yielding, adaptable

elder   senior, older, *younger*

elect   select, pick, choose, vote for

elegant   tasteful, polished, refined, cultured, fine, *vulgar, common*

element   part, aspect

elementary   basic, fundamental, introductory, beginning, simple, primary, *advanced*

elevate   raise, exalt, erect, lift, hoist, boost, *lower*

eligible   qualified, desirable, fit, suitable, *ineligible*

eliminate   throw out, remove, discard, reject, exclude, expunge, erase, *include*

else   different, other

embarrassed   ashamed, mortified, guilt-ridden, disgraced, humiliated

elevate

emblem   symbol, badge, token, mark, sign
embrace   enfold, press, hold, grasp, hug, clutch
emerge   appear, issue
emergency   pinch, crisis, calamity, disaster
emotion   sentiment, feeling, excitement, sensation
emperor   ruler, monarch, sovereign
emphasize   accent, stress, insist, highlight
employ   hire, sign on, use, engage, busy, occupy,
   fire
empress   ruler, monarch, sovereign
empty   vacant, blank, void, hollow, barren, *full*
enclosed   fenced, contained, surrounded, restricted,
   encircled, shut in, bounded, *open*

encourage   support, cheer, urge, prod, nudge, inspire,
   discourage

empty

end   stop, complete, conclude, finish, terminate,
   cease, discontinue, quit, *start*
endless   continuous, constant, nonstop, infinite,
   everlasting, perpetual, *finite*
endure   last, continue, persist, stay, remain
enemy   opponent, foe, opposition, adversary,
   antagonist, *friend, ally*
energy   power, vigor, strength, force, potency,
   vitality, might, drive
engagement   involvement, commitment
engrave   inscribe, print, carve, impress, stamp
enjoy   savor, like, relish, appreciate, *dislike*

47

enlarge   increase, expand, extend, inflate, amplify, magnify, grow, widen, *reduce, shrink*

enlist   sign up, join, enroll, register, volunteer

enormous   immense, huge, giant, gigantic, vast, colossal, large, great, *tiny*

enough   sufficient, adequate, ample, plenty, abundant, satisfactory, *insufficient*

enraged   furious, angry, mad, provoked, inflamed

enroll   register, sign up, enlist, join, involve, recruit

enter   penetrate, invade, join

entertaining   amusing, interesting, diverting, fascinating, pleasant, delightful, absorbing, *dull, boring*

enthusiastic   excited, interested, eager, keen about, *indifferent*

entire   total, complete, whole, thorough, full, *partial*

1. entrance   opening, access, door

2. entrance   charm, fascinate, bewitch, enchant

envelop   surround, enclose, encircle, wrap, embrace, cover

envious   jealous, covetous

environment   surroundings, neighborhood, atmosphere, vicinity

equal   parallel, tie, match, peer, same, *unequal*

equip   furnish, provide, supply, rig, costume, outfit

equipment   kit, gear, supplies, tools

equal

48

era   age, period, epoch, eon

erase   rub out, obliterate, cancel, cross off

erect   construct, build, raise, create

errand   assignment, chore, task, job, duty, mission

error   mistake, blunder, fallacy

escape   get away, flee, evade, avoid, dodge

escort   chaperone, accompany, guide, lead, attend, squire

especially   particularly, mainly, mostly, primarily

essay   article, composition, thesis, paper

essential   key, necessary, vital, important, fundamental, required, basic, *inessential, trivial, unimportant*

establish   set up, create, form, organize, found

estimate   judge, guess, approximate, calculate, figure, evaluate, rate, gauge

eternal   infinite, endless, everlasting, timeless

etiquette   rules of conduct, manners, formalities, amenities, courtesies

erase

evaporate   disappear, dry up, fade away, vanish

even   1. smooth, flat, level, *uneven*

even   2. uniform, same, identical, equal, *different*

evening   sunset, dusk, sundown, nightfall, gloaming

event   happening, incident, experience, occurrence, episode

eventually   ultimately, finally, at last, in time

everyday   ordinary, daily, common, usual, customary

essential

evict   turn out, throw out, expel, oust

evidence   proof, facts, clues, signs, data

evil   wicked, wrong, bad, sinful, harmful, *good*

exactly   precisely, accurately, correctly

exaggerate   overstate, magnify, stretch, overdo, *minimize*

examine   1. observe, study, inspect, scrutinize

examine   2. question, quiz, test

example   model, specimen, sample, pattern

excellent   splendid, wonderful, very good, superior, superb, *inferior*

except   leaving out, besides, barring, excluding, outside of, aside from, *including*

exceptional   unique, special, outstanding, unusual, notable, extraordinary, remarkable, *ordinary*

exchange   change, trade, switch, swap, substitute, interchange

excited

excited   enthusiastic, emotional, eager, interested, aroused, stirred, *indifferent*

excursion   outing, voyage, trip, journey, tour

1. excuse   alibi, reason

2. excuse   forgive, absolve, pardon, *blame*

executive   director, official, administrator, manager, officer

exhausted

exercise   train, drill, condition, practice, prepare

exhausted   weary, drained, fatigued, tired, used up, worn out, *energetic*

exhibit   show, flaunt, present, display, demonstrate

exile   expel, banish, cast out, deport, ban, exclude

exist   be, live, survive

existence   life, subsistence, survival, endurance

exit   go out, depart, leave, *enter*

expand   grow, enlarge, spread, broaden, increase, widen, *reduce, contract*

expect   anticipate, await, look for, hope for

expedition   trip, journey, exploration, trek, pilgrimage, voyage

expel   discharge, remove, dispose, dismiss, oust, eliminate, *admit*

expensive   dear, high-priced, costly, *cheap*

experience   happening, event, occurrence, incident, episode, adventure, sensation

experiment   test, try, prove, verify

expert   authority, specialist, master

expired   discontinued, ceased, ended, ran out

explain   simplify, describe, clarify, answer, illustrate, show, demonstrate

explode   erupt, blow up, burst

explore   search, investigate, delve into, probe, scrutinize

expose   reveal, disclose, unmask, display, uncover

express   1. swift, quick, fast, speedy, rapid, nonstop, *slow*

express   2. describe, voice, present, tell

explore

51

expression   look, air, mien

exquisite   stunning, gorgeous, beautiful, delicate, lovely, dainty, *gross*, *ugly*

extend   enlarge, stretch, reach out, increase, lengthen, broaden, expand, *contract*, *reduce*, *decrease*

exterior   outside, outer, external, surface, *interior*

exterminate   eliminate, obliterate, destroy, kill, erase, wipe out, dispose of

extinct   gone, obsolete, dead, past

extinguish   smother, put out, crush, suppress, quench

extra   surplus, spare, additional, more, supplementary

extraordinary   remarkable, exceptional, special, unusual, marvelous, noteworthy, unique, rare, *ordinary*

extreme   extravagant, excessive, exaggerated, overdone, *moderate*

extra

F

fable   legend, story, myth, fairy tale, moral tale

fabric   cloth, textile, material, goods

fabulous   spectacular, remarkable, marvelous, wonderful, splendid, superb, incredible

face   encounter, confront, meet, oppose

fact   item, point, detail, truth, certainty, evidence
factory   mill, plant, works
fad   style, craze, rage, fashion, trend
fade   lose color, dim, pale, weaken, *brighten*
fail   be unsuccessful, miscarry, lapse, flop, flunk, falter, *succeed*
faint   1. pale, hazy, weak, dim, blurred
faint   2. swoon, black out, weaken, keel over, drop
fair   1. just, right, correct, impartial, honest, square, *unfair*
fair   2. clear, sunny, bright, pleasant, *cloudy*
fair   3. ordinary, mediocre, average, *outstanding*
fair   4. pale, light, whitish, *dark*
fair   5. bazaar, carnival, festival, market, exposition
fairy   sylph, sprite, elf, pixie
faith   1. confidence, belief, trust, hope, assurance, certainty
faith   2. religion, teaching
faithful   reliable, devoted, dedicated, trustworthy, committed
fake   false, counterfeit, imitation, mock, inauthentic, *real*
fall   1. tumble, descend, plunge, drop, collapse, topple, *rise*
fall   2. autumn
false   1. incorrect, wrong, lying, untrue, *true*
false   2. counterfeit, fake, *real*

fad

fake

53

fame   reputation, renown, glory, popularity

familiar   well-known, common, popular, friendly, *strange*

family   group, folks, relatives, kin, clan, tribe

famous   well-known, notorious, renowned, celebrated, popular

fan   follower, devotee, admirer

fancy   frilly, elaborate, fussy, flowery, ornate, elegant, *plain*

fantastic   marvelous, wonderful, incredible, unusual, exceptional, remarkable, *ordinary*

far   remote, distant, removed, inaccessible, *near*

fare   tariff, toll, fee, charge, price

farm   raise, grow, cultivate, harvest, till, plow

fascinating   captivating, interesting, exciting, thrilling, absorbing, entrancing, bewitching, *boring*

fashion   1. create, shape, make, form, mold

fashion   2. style, custom, mode, vogue, trend

fast   speedy, rapid, quick, swift, hasty, *slow*

fasten   tie, secure, attach, bind, close, seal, connect, *unfasten, untie, open*

fat   plump, chubby, heavy, stout, chunky, fleshy, tubby, *thin*

fatal   deadly, lethal, mortal, killing

fate   destiny, fortune, luck

fatigue   weary, tire, exhaust

faucet   tap, spigot

familiar

fear

fault flaw, shortcoming, mistake, error, wrongdoing, misdeed

favor gift, service, good deed, kindness

favorite precious, choice, pet, prized, cherished, beloved

fear dread, fright, alarm, terror, panic

fearless bold, daring, brave, courageous, heroic, intrepid, *afraid*

feast banquet, spread

fee price, charge, fare, tariff, dues, toll

feeble frail, weak, powerless, *strong*

feed supply, nourish, nurture, sustain, satisfy

feel handle, touch, finger, grasp

feeling emotion, sensation, sympathy, passion, sentiment

female womanly, feminine, ladylike, *male, masculine*

fence 1. wall, barrier, enclosure, rail

fence 2. joust, duel, fight, parry

ferocious brutal, cruel, wild, fierce, savage, ruthless, vicious, bloodthirsty, *gentle, tame*

fertile productive, rich, fruitful, enriched, abundant, *barren*

ferocious

feud argument, fight, quarrel, battle, rivalry, controversy, squabble, bitterness

fever sickness, illness, heat, temperature, flush, excitement

fib untruth, lie, falsehood, white lie, story

fiction   story, fantasy, untruth, invention

field   tract, plot, space, land, pasture, meadow

fiend   evil spirit, devil, demon, ogre

fierce   violent, ferocious, savage, raging, vicious, wild, brutal, cruel, *gentle*

fiery   flaming, burning, hot, blazing

fiery

fight   battle, struggle, dispute, feud, quarrel, combat, contest

figure   build, physique, shape, form

file   1. group, sort, classify, categorize, put away

file   2. smooth, grind, sharpen, sand

fill   stuff, load, pack, cram, supply, *empty*

filter   screen, strain, sift, separate

filthy   dirty, polluted, soiled, grimy, mucky, *clean*

final   terminal, concluding, last, closing, *beginning*

finance   sponsor, aid, assist, subsidize, back

find   learn, discover, detect, disclose, uncover, come upon, *lose*

fine   1. splendid, excellent, good, nice

fine   2. dainty, delicate, thin, *rough, coarse*

fine   3. tax, penalize, charge

finish   end, complete, conclude, terminate, close, stop, *start*

fire   1. flame, blaze, burning

fire   2. discharge, dismiss, lay off, release, *hire*

finish

fire   3. blast, shoot, discharge

firm 1. hard, rigid, inflexible, certain, immovable, solid, steady, unmoving, *flexible, shaky*

firm 2. business, enterprise, company

fit 1. well, healthy, strong, in good shape, *unfit*

fit 2. seizure, convulsion, attack, spell, spasm

fix mend, repair, regulate, adjust, *break*

flag banner, pennant, standard, colors

flame blaze, fire

flash gleam, glare, glitter, spark

flat level, even, smooth, horizontal, *uneven*

flatter compliment, praise, honor

flavor relish, taste, tang, savor, seasoning

flee escape, run away, disappear, bolt, evade, dodge

flesh meat, body

flexible stretchable, elastic, pliable, springy, changeable, *inflexible, rigid*

flight departure, exodus, withdrawal, leaving

flimsy fragile, weak, frail, *sturdy, strong*

fling pitch, throw, cast, toss, hurl

flip toss, fling, turn over, hurl, pitch

flood overflow, overfill, overwhelm, drench, deluge

floor 1. pavement, ground, parquet

floor 2. story, level

flop drop, sag, droop, slump, fall, sink

flower bloom, flourish, blossom, develop, thrive

fluid flowing, watery, liquid, *solid*

fly glide, soar, coast, sail, wing

flexible

focus   adjust, concentrate

foe   opponent, enemy, adversary, *friend, ally*

foggy   cloudy, hazy, smoggy, dim, smoky, misty, blurred, *clear*

fold   crease, bend, double over, pleat, wrinkle, *unfold*

follow   1. trail, chase, pursue, track, trace, *lead, precede*

follow   2. use, obey, act according to, practice, *disregard, ignore*

fondness   affection, love, liking, warmth

foolish   silly, dumb, stupid, senseless, ridiculous, idiotic

forbid   bar, prevent, ban, prohibit, deter, *allow*

force   1. drive, pressure, make, push, compel, oblige

force   2. strength, energy, might, power, vigor

forecast   prophecy, prediction, foretelling

foreign   stranger, alien, external

forget   overlook, neglect, disregard, ignore

forgive   excuse, pardon, absolve, release, *blame*

forlorn   downcast, sad, despondent, melancholy, hopeless, deserted, abandoned, forsaken

form   develop, fashion, shape, make, construct, create, mold

forlorn

formal   conventional, orderly, regular, *informal, casual*

fortunate   lucky, *unlucky*

fortune 1. riches, wealth, treasure

fortune 2. luck, chance, fate, destiny

forward ahead, onward, advance, *backward*

foundation 1. ground, base

foundation 2. organization, institution, establishment

fraction segment, piece, part, portion, division

fracture shatter, crack, split, break, smash, rupture, *heal*

fracture

fragile breakable, brittle, delicate, frail

frail delicate, slight, fragile, weak, dainty, *strong*

frame edge, border, trim, boundary

frantic hysterical, excited, wild, violent, upset, delirious, frenzied, desperate, *calm*

fraud cheating, trickery, swindle, dishonesty

freak grotesque, unusual, bizarre, queer, incredible

free 1. liberate, release, dismiss, discharge, clear, acquit, deliver, emancipate, *enslave*, *restrain*

free 2. complimentary, without charge, gratis

freedom liberty, independence, *bondage*, *slavery*

freeze chill, ice, harden, stiffen

frequently repeatedly, regularly, often, commonly, *seldom*

fresh vigorous, healthy, unused, firsthand, *stale*

fret fuss, bother, worry

friend buddy, pal, comrade, companion, intimate, mate, chum, *enemy*

friend

friendship closeness, intimacy, partnership, companionship

frighten terrify, alarm, scare, shock

frosting topping, icing

frosty frigid, freezing, icy, cold, *hot*

frown scowl, grimace, pout

frozen frigid, frosty, icy, cold

frustrated balked, baffled, foiled, discouraged, defeated

full heaping, packed, overflowing, stuffed, loaded, jammed, crammed, crowded, *empty*

fun entertainment, pleasure, amusement, enjoyment

funny entertaining, amusing, humorous, comical, laughable, *sad*

fur skin, hide, pelt

furious mad, infuriated, enraged, angry, annoyed, rabid, upset, *calm*

furnish provide, equip, supply, outfit, give

fuse join, blend, unite, melt, combine, glue, weld, *separate*

fuss hubbub, commotion, worry, bother

future tomorrow, hereafter, *past*

fuzz fluff, fur, down

frustrated

G

gadget

gadget tool, contraption, appliance, device, utensil, implement

gag joke, jest

gain get, obtain, earn, receive, acquire

gallant chivalrous, heroic, brave, courteous, valiant, fearless

gallop run, spring, trot, canter

gamble risk, wager, bet, speculate

gang pack, crew, bunch, troop, crowd, mob, band

gap hole, opening, space, break

garbage waste, trash, junk, refuse, debris, rubbish, litter

garden cultivate, plant, raise, grow, harvest

gash wound, laceration, cut

gate barrier, fence

garbage

gather amass, accumulate, collect, assemble, compile, cluster, *scatter*

gay 1. jolly, cheerful, happy, lively, merry, *glum*

gay 2. vivid, colorful, bright, *dull*

gaze gape, gawk, stare

gem precious stone, jewel, treasure

general commander, officer, leader

generous unselfish, giving, big-hearted, liberal, kind, openhanded, *selfish*

genius

genius   prodigy, master

gentle   mild, soft, soothing, tender, kindly, *rough, harsh*

genuine   real, authentic, true, pure, legitimate, *fake*

germ   seed, origin, beginning, microbe, bug

get   receive, obtain, fetch, bring

ghost   phantom, spirit, specter, spook

giant   gigantic, enormous, colossal, huge, vast, mammoth, immense, monumental, *tiny*

gift   1. offering, present, donation, contribution

gift   2. ability, talent, endowment, power, aptitude, forte

gigantic   giant, huge, colossal, vast, immense, enormous, mammoth, monumental, *tiny*

giggle   chuckle, laugh, titter, snicker

give   hand over, present, offer, bestow, donate, provide, allot, *take*

glacier   iceberg

glad   pleased, cheerful, happy, joyful, delighted, satisfied, contented, *unhappy*

glamorous   stunning, gorgeous, beautiful, attractive, dazzling, elegant, entrancing, *unattractive*

glance   glimpse, look, gaze

glare   scowl, stare, glower

glaring   bright, blinding, shining, glowing, flaring

glaze   gloss, buff, polish, wax, coat, cover

glamorous

gleaming   glowing, bright, shining, beaming, sparkling, glittering, *dim*

glide   slide, skim, move easily, cruise, flow, coast, sail

glitter   glisten, sparkle, shine

globe   sphere, world, planet, Earth

gloomy   dismal, dreary, dim, dark, depressing, bleak, *cheerful*

glorious   magnificent, splendid, wonderful, great, divine, marvelous, grand, superb, majestic

glowing   beaming, sparkling, gleaming, bright, shining, blazing

glue   cement, paste, fasten, stick together

glum   gloomy, sad, moody, depressed, sullen, *cheerful*

gnaw   chew, gnash, grind

goal   object, purpose, aim, target, end, destination

gobble   devour, gulp, swallow, gorge, stuff

good   decent, fine, right, nice, proper, appropriate, admirable, *bad*, *evil*

gobble

gorgeous   lovely, stunning, beautiful, glorious, dazzling, ravishing, pretty, *ugly*

gossip   rumors, chatter, tattle

govern   regulate, command, rule, control, lead, supervise, manage, head, direct, run, preside, guide

grab   seize, snatch, clutch, grasp, grip

gracious   courteous, cordial, polite, pleasant, kindly, friendly, generous, hospitable, *rude*, *unkind*

grade   1. score, mark, rate, evaluate

grade   2. division, class, category, group, standard

gradual   slow, easy, step-by-step

graduate   advance, pass, succeed, matriculate

grand   stately, glorious, magnificent, majestic, great, splendid, dignified

grant   1. contribute, give, donate, present, award, bestow

grant   2. permit, allow, accept, *deny*

grasp   snatch, seize, grab, grip, clutch, hold, apprehend, *release*

grate   scrape, grind, file, scratch, annoy

grateful   appreciative, thankful, obliged, *ungrateful*

grave   plot, burial place

gravel   pebbles, stones

grease   lubrication, fat, oil

great   magnificent, grand, large, outstanding, famous, distinguished, important, sensational, remarkable, *ordinary*

greedy   selfish, piggish, avaricious, miserly

greet   welcome, hail, address, salute

grieve   mourn, lament, sorrow

grim   stern, harsh, fierce

grimy   filthy, dirty, soiled, sooty, smutty, gritty, *clean*

grin   smile, beam, smirk

grind   mash, squash, crush, crumble, pulverize, grate, rub

greet

grin

64

grip   clutch, hold, clasp, grasp, seize, clench

groan   moan, wail, howl

grope   fumble, touch, feel

gross   vulgar, coarse, crude, unrefined, *refined*

grotesque   bizarre, deformed, ugly, disfigured, monstrous, ill-shaped

grouchy   cranky, crabby, cross, irritable, disagreeable, grumpy, moody

ground   dirt, earth, soil, floor, land

group   classify, sort, organize, arrange, assemble

grow   1. age, increase, rise, develop, mature, progress, advance, gain, *shrink*

grow   2. raise, plant, farm, cultivate, harvest

growl   grumble, snarl, complain

grown-up   mature, adult

grumpy   grouchy, cranky, crabby, bad-tempered

guarantee   warrant, promise, pledge, assure, certify

guard   protect, defend, watch over, secure, patrol, shield, police

growl

guardian   supervisor, protector, trustee

guess   suppose, estimate, approximate, figure, imagine, think, assume, believe, conjecture

guest   company, visitor, caller

guide   1. point out, lead, show, direct, steer, escort, squire, conduct

guide   2. regulate, control, direct, manage, advise, govern, rule

guilty   at fault, criminal, blameworthy, culpable
gun   firearm, weapon, revolver, pistol
gymnastics   calisthenics, exercises, athletics, acrobatics

H

hair

habit   practice, custom, trait, pattern
hack   chop, cut, sever, slice, split
hair   tresses, locks, curls
hall   1. passageway, corridor, lobby, foyer
hall   2. auditorium, meeting room, theater
halt   stop, quit, end, terminate, conclude, cease, *start*
hammer   1. knock, hit, pound, bang, beat
hammer   2. mallet
hand   deliver, give, transfer, transmit, pass, turn over
handbag   pocketbook, purse, bag
handicap   disadvantage, hindrance, burden, *asset*
handle   1. finger, touch, feel, manipulate, use
handle   2. take care of, run, direct, manage, regulate, govern
handsome   attractive, good-looking, *ugly*
handwriting   penmanship, script

handy 1. nearby, useful, convenient, ready, available, *inconvenient*

handy 2. apt, adept, skilled, clever, expert, *inept*, *clumsy*

hang suspend, fasten, dangle, droop, sag

happen take place, occur, come off

happy contented, cheerful, jolly, joyful, glad, gay, satisfied, pleased, fulfilled, *unhappy*, *sad*

happy

harbor dock, port, wharf, pier

hard 1. stiff, rigid, firm, solid, stony, unyielding, *soft*

hard 2. rough, difficult, tough, rugged, *easy*

hardly scarcely, barely, nearly, narrowly

hardy tough, strong, sturdy, rugged, robust, healthy, powerful, *weak*, *frail*

harm damage, hurt, impair, injure, wrong

harmful dangerous, injurious

harmless innocent, blameless

harmony accord, agreement, unity, compatibility

harsh severe, cruel, hard, gruff, stern, rough, curt, tough, grating, brusque, sharp, bitter

hardy

harvest yield, output, crop

hasty 1. speedy, quick, rapid, swift, hurried, fleet, *slow*

hasty 2. reckless, rash, impetuous, impulsive, *planned*, *considered*

hatch generate, breed, produce, incubate

hate loathe, abominate, dislike, despise, detest, abhor, *love*

haul pull, drag, tow, tug, draw

haunted eerie, weird, spooky, possessed, ghost-ridden

hazardous unsafe, dangerous, risky, harmful, *safe*

hazy 1. dim, cloudy, misty, foggy, smoky, overcast, *clear*

hazy 2. uncertain, confused, fuzzy, vague, blurred, *clear*

head command, lead, direct, manage, control, run, supervise, govern

heading headline, title, topic, theme

headquarters main office, base, center

heal cure, mend, repair, correct, remedy, restore

health well-being

heaping overflowing, loaded, piled, stuffed, stacked, full

hear listen, heed, take in

heat warmth, excitement, fire, fever

heavy plump, hefty, chubby, husky, fat, stout, burdensome *light, thin*

hectic busy, frantic, exciting, stirring, *calm*

help assist, aid, support, cooperate, benefit, relieve, *hinder*

helpful cooperative, beneficial, useful, of assistance

hem edge, border, rim

help

heroic

heroic fearless, courageous, valiant, brave, bold, gallant, *cowardly*

hesitate falter, waver, flounder

hide cover, conceal, camouflage, mask, enclose, bury, *reveal*

hideous horrible, ugly, ghastly, wretched, awful, dreadful, repellent, revolting, *beautiful*

high tall, lofty, steep, towering, elevated, soaring, *low*

highway expressway, freeway, road, turnpike, thoroughfare

hike walk, tramp, march, parade

hilarious humorous, comic, amusing, laughable, funny

hilarious

hint suggestion, clue, implication

hire 1. engage, take on, employ, *fire*

hire 2. rent, lease, charter

history record, chronicle, annals, story

hit smack, strike, bat, slug, swat, slap, punch, poke, crack

hoist boost, elevate, raise, lift

hole opening, gap, cavity, void

hollow vacant, empty, bare, blank, barren

holy sacred, pure, spiritual, consecrated

home house, dwelling, hearth, residence, abode, habitat

homely   unattractive, plain, ugly, unappealing, *attractive*

honest   truthful, sincere, moral, ethical, upright, honorable, fair

hood   cover, lid, veil, cap

hook   latch, snap, clasp, fasten, clip, bind, attach, *unhook*

hoot   yell, call, cry, shriek

hope   desire, yearn, expect, wish, pray

hopeless   impossible, insoluble, desperate

horizontal   level, even, flat, plane, *vertical*

horrible   awful, dreadful, frightful, terrible, wretched, ghastly, horrid

horse   steed, mount, mare, stallion, colt, filly

hostile   unfriendly, bitter, aggressive, belligerent, antagonistic

hot

hot   1. sizzling, torrid, steaming, blazing, sweltering, *cold*

hot   2. sharp, spicy, tangy, peppery, nippy, *bland*

house   home, shelter, residence, dwelling, abode, habitat

howl   shriek, cry, yell, shout, scream, screech, wail, yowl

hubbub   commotion, noise, ruckus, fuss, clamor, disturbance, tumult, excitement, *calm, stillness*

howl

huddle   cluster, crowd, assemble, gather

hug hold, grasp, embrace, squeeze, clutch, cuddle, press, enfold

huge enormous, gigantic, immense, vast, mammoth, giant, monumental, tremendous, *tiny*

hum drone, buzz

humble meek, modest, simple, plain, unpretentious, *showy*

humid damp, moist, muggy, wet, *dry*

humiliated mortified, ashamed, embarrassed, disgraced

humorous comic, laughable, funny, witty, clever

hump bump, ridge, bulge

hunger craving, appetite, desire, eagerness

hunk lump, piece, mass, chunk, gob, wad

hunt search, seek, scout, explore

hurl throw, toss, pitch, fling, cast

hurry hasten, rush, accelerate, hustle, speed

hurt harm, impair, injure, damage, bruise, wound

husband mate, spouse, married man

husky rugged, sturdy, muscular, strong, athletic, stocky, *slight*

hustle hasten, rush, bustle, speed

hut shed, shack, cabin, shanty

hypnotize spellbind, entrance, mesmerize

hysterical delirious, frantic, overexcited, upset, wild, frenzied, *calm*

hypnotize

71

I

ice   sleet, hail, frozen water

icing   topping, frosting

idea   notion, thought, concept, opinion

ideal   perfect, model, flawless

identify   name, tag, label, recognize, describe, distinguish

idiot   moron, fool, imbecile, simpleton, half-wit, dunce, blockhead

idle   lazy, inactive, unoccupied

ignore   overlook, avoid, snub, shun, disregard

ill   infirm, sick, ailing, *healthy*

idle

illegal   unlawful, illegitimate, criminal, fraudulent, *legal*

illustrate   draw, portray, picture, show, demonstrate

image   representation, likeness, picture, vision, appearance

imaginary   untrue, envisioned, fictional

imagine   1. suppose, believe, think, guess, presume

imagine   2. speculate, fantasize, dream, envision

imbecile   blockhead, moron, half-wit, idiot, dunce, fool, simpleton

imitate   repeat, copy, mirror, duplicate, reflect

immature   undeveloped, unripe, childish, inexperienced

imitate

immediately   instantly, now, right away, promptly, at once, *later*

immense   gigantic, giant, huge, enormous, vast, colossal, monumental, *tiny*

immortal   eternal, undying, everlasting

immune   resistant, exempt, spared, excused

impatient   edgy, restless, anxious, intolerant, *patient*

impolite   rude, discourteous, ill-mannered, disrespectful, insolent, *polite*

important   essential, necessary, meaningful, urgent, significant, major, central, *unimportant, trivial*

impatient

impose   put, place, charge, force, burden with

impossible   inconceivable, unimaginable, unthinkable, absurd, *possible, likely*

impostor   pretender, deceiver, phony, fake, fraud

impress   affect, strike, imprint

impression   idea, assumption, opinion, sensation

improper   wrong, incorrect, unsuitable, inappropriate

improve   better, advance, perfect, ameliorate

incident   happening, event, episode, occurrence

incinerator   burner, furnace

include   cover, contain, comprise, *exclude*

income   pay, salary, earnings, wages, proceeds

incomplete   unfinished, deficient, wanting, partial, lacking, *complete*

inconsiderate   unkind, ungracious, thoughtless, rude, *considerate*

73

incorrect   faulty, wrong, inaccurate, mistaken, improper, *correct*

increase   expand, extend, enlarge, inflate, magnify, *decrease*

incredible   unbelievable, fantastic, absurd, inconceivable

independent   1. acting alone, autonomous, self-reliant, *dependent*

independent   2. impartial, unbiased, neutral, disinterested

indicate   point out, show, express, demonstrate, signify, suggest, imply

indistinct   cloudy, vague, unclear, dim, blurred, hazy, obscure, *distinct*, *clear*

individual   single, separate, personal, special

indulge   humor, favor, pamper, coddle, cater to

industry   trade, business, labor, dealings

inexpensive   low-priced, cheap, low-cost, reasonable, *expensive*

infect   contaminate, poison, pollute, corrupt

inferior   lower, lesser, subordinate, secondary, worse

infinite   endless, limitless, boundless, eternal

inflate   expand, swell, stretch, *deflate*

inflexible   stiff, rigid, firm, immovable, *flexible*

influence   persuade, sway, move, induce

inform   notify, tell, instruct, communicate, report, enlighten

inflate

information knowledge, data, news, facts, communications

infuriate enrage, antagonize, anger, upset, irritate, provoke, madden, *soothe*

ingredient element, part, component, factor

inhabit live, dwell, occupy, stay

inherit receive, come into

initial first, beginning, early, introductory

injure hurt, harm, impair, damage, bruise, wrong

injustice inequity, unfairness

inn lodge, motel, hotel, tavern, roadhouse

inner interior, hidden, covered, *outer*

innocent without guilt, faultless, blameless, sinless, harmless, *guilty*

inquire question, investigate, ask, probe

inquisitive prying, snooping, nosy, curious

insane deranged, mad, unbalanced, crazy, *sane*

insert enter, insinuate, inject, introduce

insignia symbols, emblems, badges

insist demand, urge, press, push, stress

inspect study, examine, review, observe

inspire encourage, influence, cause, prompt

instantly immediately, promptly, fast, quickly, swiftly, rapidly

instinct natural feeling, innate tendency, predisposition

ingredient

insignia

institution establishment, association, organization, group

instruct educate, teach, tell, inform, show, direct, advise

instrument implement, device, tool, utensil, gadget, means, appliance

insult affront, humiliate, offend

insurance protection, guarantee, safeguard, shelter

intelligent smart, bright, wise, alert, sensible, rational, *ignorant*

intend mean, plan, propose, aim

interest concern, curiosity, intrigue

interesting amusing, entertaining, fascinating, captivating, absorbing, provocative, *uninteresting, boring*

interfere meddle, obstruct, intrude

intermission pause, recess, interval, interlude, break, respite

interpret explain, restate, clarify

interrupt interfere, intrude, break in

interview question, interrogate, quiz, examine

introduce launch, inaugurate, innovate

intrude meddle, interfere, trespass

invade attack, raid, overrun, trespass

invalid weak, unhealthy, frail, infirm, sickly, ailing, *healthy*

intelligent

invent   originate, develop, produce, make up, create, devise, discover, contrive

investigate   examine, explore, inspect, look into, probe, study, scrutinize

invisible   unseen, hidden, out of sight, *exposed*

invite   call, ask, request, summon

involve   include, implicate, encompass, envelop, concern, affect

irregular   unnatural, abnormal, erratic, rough, unusual

irritable   cranky, cross, grouchy, annoyed, impatient, grumpy, disagreeable, bad-tempered, *good-humored*, *pleasant*

irritate   1. anger, infuriate, annoy, bother, provoke, disturb

irritate   2. chafe, rub, grate, inflame, *soothe*

isolate   separate, quarantine, segregate, seclude

issue   1. theme, subject, topic, question, point, matter

issue   2. edition, copy, number, volume

item   part, segment, piece, article, entry

invent

investigate

J

jab

jab poke, thrust, push, prod

jagged pointy, ragged, notched

jail imprison, incarcerate, lock up

jam 1. stuff, crowd, squeeze, cram, crush, pack

jam 2. jelly, preserve, marmalade

janitor custodian, caretaker

jealous envious, covetous

jerk yank, pull, jolt, tug

jewel gem, ornament, stone

job task, employment, work, duty, chore,
assignment, position, occupation, business

jog sprint, run, trot

join unite, link, connect, attach, fasten, combine,
detach, separate

joke jest, tease, quip, banter

jolly jovial, merry, pleasant, happy, gay, cheerful,
good-spirited, *glum*

jolt jar, shake, startle, bump

journey excursion, trip, expedition, pilgrimage, tour,
voyage

joyful happy, ecstatic, jovial, jolly, merry, cheerful,
gay, glad, *glum*

judge umpire, referee, mediator

judgment opinion, ruling, verdict, assessment

WHY DID THE HUMAN
CROSS THE ROAD?

joke

jumbo

jumble   scramble, mix, confuse, muddle
jumbo   giant, gigantic, colossal, enormous, immense, huge, mammoth, *tiny*
jump   leap, spring, pounce, bound
junior   younger, lower, lesser, *senior*
junk   trash, rubbish, garbage, scrap
just   fair, moral, right, proper, impartial, unbiased, *unjust*
juvenile   youthful, young, immature, *old*, *mature*

K

keep   preserve, conserve, save, retain, *discard*
kennel   pound, doghouse
key   1. evidence, hint, clue, lead, answer, explanation
key   2. note, tone, pitch, scale
kick   push, prod, nudge, jar
kid   1. fool, tease, jest, joke, josh
kid   2. tot, child, infant
kidnap   abduct, snatch, carry off
kill   murder, slay, slaughter, execute, assassinate, annihilate

kiss

kind 1. thoughtful, considerate, loving, sympathetic, generous, gentle, helpful, *unkind*, *mean*

kind 2. type, sort, variety, species

king chief, monarch, ruler, sovereign, potentate

kiss buss, peck, smack

kit gear, set, furnishings, equipment, outfit

knack ability, skill, talent, know-how

knife blade, sword

knit weave, sew, fasten, connect, unite, blend, unify

knock punch, rap, beat, hit, strike, hammer, bang

knot tangle

know understand, comprehend, perceive, recognize, grasp

knowledge wisdom, information, understanding

L

label name, tag, title

labor toil, work, industry, employment

lack need, want, require, fall short

ladle scoop, dipper

lady woman, matron, female

lag linger, loiter, delay, dawdle, tarry

lagoon marsh, swamp, pool, bay

lame crippled, injured, limping

land touch down, arrive, descend, alight

lane road, path, alley, aisle, avenue, channel

language tongue, speech, words, talk

lap lick, sip, drink

large huge, big, enormous, tremendous, grand, immense, massive, giant, colossal, *small*

lariat lasso, rope, line

last end, final, ultimate, concluding, *beginning*, *first*

latch clasp, hook, lock, fastener, closing

late tardy, behind, slow

late

lather suds, foam, soap, froth

laugh chuckle, titter, giggle, guffaw

launch introduce, begin, start, establish, set afloat

launder wash, scrub, clean, scour

law rule, principle, act, regulation, ordinance, decree, edict

lawyer attorney, counselor, solicitor

lay place, put, set, deposit

layer stratum, slice, level

lazy idle, lax, inactive, indolent, *active*

lead manage, conduct, guide, direct, head, escort, steer

leader manager, guide, director, chief, head

league group, union, alliance, association, society

leak drip, dribble

lazy

leap   spring, jump, bound, pounce

learn   discover, absorb, find out, memorize

lease   hire, rent, charter

leash   strap, rein, shackle, chain

least   fewest, minimum, smallest, *most, maximum*

leave   1. depart, go, exit, withdraw, vacate, *arrive*

leave   2. abandon, quit, desert, *stay*

lecture   address, sermon, speech, talk, recitation, oration

ledge   shelf, edge, rim

left   abandoned, remaining

legal   lawful, authorized, admissible, permitted, allowed, legitimate, just, valid, *illegal*

legend   myth, fairy tale, fable, story, folklore

lend   loan, give, advance, *borrow*

lengthen

lengthen   stretch, prolong, extend, draw out, *shorten*

less   fewer, smaller, reduced, *more*

lessen   reduce, constrain, compress, condense

lesson   instruction, exercise, teaching, assignment, course

liberty

let   allow, permit, consent, grant, admit

letter   note, message, communication

level   even, flat, smooth, uniform, *uneven*

liar   fibber, fraud, deceiver

liberty   freedom, emancipation, independence, autonomy

license   consent, sanction, approval, permission, warrant, authorization

lid   top, cap, cover

lie   fib, falsify, exaggerate, fabricate

lifeless   dull, limp, *vital*

lift   elevate, raise, boost, hoist, pick up, *lower*

light   1. clear, bright, open, lucid, *dark*

light   2. airy, weightless, delicate, *heavy*

like   admire, appreciate, enjoy, prefer, *dislike*

limit   restriction, end, boundary, extreme, tip

limp   drooping, sagging, loose, weak, soft

link   connect, join, combine, attach, unite, bridge, couple, tie, *separate*

liquid   fluid, watery, *solid*

list   enumerate, record, inventory

listen   hear, eavesdrop

literature   writings, books, stories, information

litter   garbage, rubbish, junk, trash, scrap, clutter

live   reside, dwell, inhabit, occupy

lively   dynamic, animated, active, energetic, vivacious, vivid, spry, spirited, *dull*

load   1. cargo, burden, freight

load   2. pack, stuff, fill, *unload, empty*

loaf   lounge, idle, loiter

loan   lend, give, advance

lobby   foyer, vestibule, entrance, hallway

local   regional, limited, particular, restricted

light

lock

locate   find, discover, identify

location   place, area, spot, site, neighborhood, region, position

lock   hook, close, fasten, latch, clasp, shut, seal, *unlock, open*

logical   sensible, rational, reasonable, sound, sane, *illogical*

lonely   solitary, friendless, alone, isolated

long   lengthy, enduring, extensive, *short*

look   1. see, glance, gaze, stare, peek, peer, gape

look   2. appear, seem

loose   slack, unfastened, limp, drooping, *tight*

lose   1. flop, fail, forfeit, sacrifice, *win*

lose   2. mislay, misplace, *find*

lotion   ointment, cream, salve

lottery   drawing, raffle

loud   roaring, noisy, thunderous, resounding, *soft*

love   cherish, idolize, adore, admire, care for, *hate*

lovely   pleasing, attractive, delightful, pretty, gorgeous, charming, beautiful, appealing, exquisite, *unattractive*

low   inferior, short, lesser, *high*

loyal   faithful, devoted, true, obedient, trustworthy, dutiful, *disloyal*

lucky   fortunate, happy, *unhappy*

lug   drag, pull, tug, carry, haul

luggage   baggage, suitcases, bags, valises

loyal

lump swelling, bump, hump, chunk, mass
luxurious prosperous, elegant, extravagant, magnificent, comfortable, grand, splendid

M

machine equipment, mechanism, appliance
mad 1. insane, deranged, crazy, lunatic, *sane*
mad 2. enraged, furious, annoyed, angry, irritated, cross, upset, exasperated, ornery
magazine journal, periodical, publication
magic sorcery, wizardry, witchcraft, voodoo
magnetic alluring, attractive, pulling, drawing, entrancing, enticing
magnificent splendid, luxurious, stately, grand, glorious, exquisite, superb, wonderful, marvelous, fabulous, fantastic
magnify enlarge, inflate, amplify, increase, expand, exaggerate, blow up, widen
maid servant, domestic, housekeeper, helper
mail 1. post, send, dispatch
mail 2. correspondence, letters

maid

majestic

main principal, chief, primary, foremost, leading, dominant, major

maintain keep, uphold, possess, support, preserve, retain

majestic grand, stately, noble, dignified, regal, kingly, impressive, imposing

major main, central, leading, greater, superior, larger, *minor*

make 1. compose, construct, build, create, fabricate, manufacture, produce, form, assemble

make 2. cause, force, compel

make 3. type, sort, brand, line, kind

male masculine, manly, *female, feminine*

manage direct, conduct, guide, lead, run, supervise, control, operate, regulate, govern

manager chief, director, head, supervisor

manner way, custom, style, character, nature, method

manual handbook, guidebook, directory

manufacture build, make, produce, create, construct, form, assemble, fabricate

many several, numerous, various, multitudinous, *few*

map chart

marathon race, contest

march hike, parade, walk, tramp

margin edge, rim, border, leeway, room

marionette puppet, doll

mark   rating, grade

market   shop, store, bazaar

marry   wed, join, couple, unite

marvelous   fabulous, wonderful, great, grand, exceptional, splendid, magnificent, superb, divine, sensational, spectacular, glorious, miraculous, *ordinary*

mash   smash, crumble, pulverize, grind, crush

mask   camouflage, disguise, cover, hide

masquerade   pretend, disguise, impersonate, pose

mass   bunch, bulk, lump, quantity, lots, batch, heap

master   chief, head, commander, ruler, director

match   game, contest, battle, encounter

mate   pair, couple, team

masquerade

material   substance, fabric, goods, stuff

mature   grown-up, adult, full-grown, developed, ripe, *immature*

maximum   greatest, largest, most, highest, *minimum*

maybe   possibly, perhaps, conceivably

maze   labyrinth, tangle, network, confusion

meadow   field, pasture, grassland, range

mean   1. imply, suggest, signify, convey

mean   2. nasty, unkind, malicious, cross, cruel, petty, *kind*

measure   size, grade, assess, rank, appraise, compare, rate

mechanic   technician, repairperson, machinist

mechanic

medal   prize, award, trophy, honor, medallion

medicine   drug, remedy, cure, potion, lotion, pill

medium   middle, average, mean

meek   humble, shy, tame, timid, mild, modest, gentle, *aggressive*

meet   gather, congregate, assemble, converge, encounter

melody   song, tune

melt   dissolve, soften, liquefy

memory   recollection, remembrance, recall

menace   danger, threat, warning

mend   repair, fix, adjust, regulate, heal, cure, *break*

merchandise   products, wares, goods, commodities

merchant   dealer, buyer, seller, storekeeper, trader

mercy   clemency, pity, sympathy, compassion

merge   fuse, unite, combine, mix, blend, join, mingle, *separate*

merry   happy, lively, gay, jolly, mirthful, cheerful, jovial, *glum*

mess   clutter, disorder, disarray, dirt

message   report, word, dispatch, communication, letter, note

messy   careless, untidy, sloppy, dirty, disorganized, disordered, *neat*, *tidy*

meter   measure, gauge, record

method   manner, plan, system, means, style, way, procedure, mode, fashion

OINK!

messy

88

microscopic infinitesimal, minute, tiny, *huge*
middle center, core, hub, heart, nucleus
mighty powerful, strong, grand, great, potent, *weak*
mild calm, gentle, temperate, moderate, *harsh*
military troops, army, armed forces, soldiers, service, militia

mighty

mimic imitate, mime, copy, parrot, mock, ape
mind 1. intelligence, intellect, brain, reason
mind 2. care for, look after, watch, tend
miniature tiny, small, minute, small-scale, *giant*
minimum smallest, least, lowest, *maximum*
minister pastor, clergyman, chaplain
minor smaller, lesser, inferior, secondary, lower, *major*
1. minute moment, instant, twinkling
2. minute miniature, tiny, small, slight, negligible, *giant*
miraculous marvelous, wonderful, remarkable, awesome, incredible, extraordinary, unbelievable
mirror reflect, echo, copy, imitate
mischievous devilish, playful, naughty, impish
miserable 1. unhappy, sad, downcast, depressed, *happy*

mirror

miserable 2. mean, shabby, wretched, *pleasant*
misfortune calamity, mishap, trouble, difficulty, sorrow
mislead trick, dupe, deceive, misdirect

misplace   mislay, lose, miss

missile   projectile, rocket

missing   gone, lost, absent, vanished, *present*

mission   task, errand, job, assignment, calling

mistake   fault, blunder, error, slip, oversight

mistreat   molest, abuse, manhandle

misty   foggy, cloudy, smoky, hazy, *clear*

misunderstanding   disagreement, difference, difficulty, mistake, error

mix   combine, stir, blend, fuse, mingle, merge, scramble, *separate*

mixture   blending, combination, concoction

moan   wail, howl, groan, cry, complain

mob   bunch, crowd, pack, horde, throng

mock   mimic, tease, ape, parrot, ridicule, scoff, jeer, taunt

modest

model   likeness, duplicate, replica, reproduction, image

modern   contemporary, up-to-date, new, advanced, recent, current, *old-fashioned*

modest   meek, bashful, humble, quiet, shy, *bold, arrogant*

moist   soggy, wet, damp, humid, *dry*

mold   1. form, shape, model, carve

mold   2. rot, decay, disintegrate, deteriorate, spoil

molest   abuse, harm, annoy, torment, badger, mistreat

moist

90

moment   instant, twinkling, minute

monarch   king, sovereign, ruler, emperor, queen, chief, empress

money   cash, coins, currency

monitor   assistant, helper, proctor

monotonous   tedious, humdrum, boring, dull, uninteresting, *interesting*, *varied*

money

monster   demon, ogre, fiend, freak, giant

monument   tower, memorial, shrine

mood   feeling, disposition, temperament, humor

moody   sullen, changeable, gloomy, depressed, temperamental

mop   swab, wash, scrub, wipe

motion   activity, movement, stir

mountain   hill, peak, elevation

mourn   grieve, sorrow, lament, bewail, bemoan

movement   motion, animation, activity

movie   film

mow   crop, clip, cut, trim, shear

mud   dirt, muck, slime, slush, mire

muggy   moist, damp, humid, sticky, dank

mumble   mutter, grumble, murmur

murder   assassinate, kill, slaughter, execute, wipe out

mute   dumb, speechless, silent

mutiny   uprising, riot, revolt, rebellion, insurrection

mystery   puzzle, secret, problem

myth   legend, fable, story, fairy tale, fantasy, falsehood

N

HOW COULD YOU FORGET THE MILK?...BRING ME BACK SOME MILK OR ELSE!!

nag

nag   bother, annoy, pick on, pester

nail   attach, fasten, secure, fix, hold

naked   nude, uncovered, bare, undressed, bald, *covered*

name   title, tag, label

nap   drowse, doze, sleep, snooze, drop off

narcotics   opiates, drugs, painkillers

narrator   storyteller, reporter

narrow   limited, confined, cramped, close, restricted, tight

nasty   disgusting, petty, unpleasant, repulsive, foul, odious, offensive, obnoxious, mean, *delightful*, *pleasant*

nation   homeland, land, principality, country

native   natural, original, *foreign*

natural   pure, real, genuine, unaffected, *artificial*

naturally   surely, of course, unquestionably, certainly

naughty   disobedient, bad, disorderly, mischievous, *obedient*, *good*

naughty

navigate   steer, guide

near   at hand, close, imminent

nearly   close to, almost, approximately

neat   well-kept, orderly, tidy, trim, shipshape, *sloppy*, *messy*

necessary   essential, required, basic, needed, important, urgent, fundamental, *unnecessary*

need   lack, want, require

neglected   disregarded, overlooked, ignored, slighted

neighborhood   community, area, vicinity, surroundings, environment

nerve   daring, courage, strength, bravado

nervous   anxious, restless, upset, disturbed, jittery, tense, edgy, shaken, fearful, flustered, strained, high-strung, *calm*

nestle   snuggle, cuddle, hug

net   trap, snare

network   system, maze, connection

neutral   fair, detached, impartial, unbiased, independent

new   up-to-date, current, modern, fresh, recent, original, young, *old*

news   tidings, information, broadcast, announcement

newspaper   journal, periodical, publication

nibble   munch, chew, taste, sample

nice   agreeable, pleasant, fine, good, gratifying, *unpleasant*

noble   great, grand, lofty, eminent, uplifting, honorable, stately, aristocratic

nod   bow, bob, signal, tip, bend

noise   commotion, clamor, racket, sounds, clatter, uproar, tumult, *quiet*

GULP!

nervous

nominate   select, name, designate, choose, elect

nonsense   foolishness, rubbish, stupidity, absurdity

normal   usual, standard, typical, regular, ordinary, average, *abnormal*, *unusual*

Really?...you must be joking!

nosy

nosy   prying, curious, snoopy, inquisitive

note   message, memo, jotting

notebook   tablet, pad, journal, diary

notice   observe, see, heed, note

notify   inform, advise, announce, tell, enlighten

notion   idea, view, belief, opinion

now   instantly, right away, at once, immediately, promptly, *later*

nudge   prod, push, encourage, prompt, inspire, nag, urge

nuisance   annoyance, bother, pest, disturbance

numb   deadened, unfeeling, dull, insensitive

number   1. count, quantity, sum, amount

number   2. numeral, symbol, figure, digit

numeral   number, symbol, digit, figure

numerous   a lot, several, lots, many, various, abundant

nurse   nurture, foster, care for, tend to

nutrition   nourishment, food

O

oath   promise, pledge, vow, commitment

obey   heed, submit, listen to, mind, comply, *disobey*

1. object   1. article, item, thing, entity

   object   2. aim, goal, target, purpose, intent

2. object   resist, disagree, protest, complain, challenge, disapprove, *agree*, *approve*

obligation   duty, requirement, commitment

obnoxious   disgusting, unpleasant, nasty, disagreeable, hateful, offensive, repulsive, vile, wretched, despicable, *agreeable*, *pleasant*

obnoxious

observe   watch, look, see, perceive, note, examine, study

obstacle   obstruction, block, snag, barrier, hindrance

obstinate   willful, stubborn, inflexible, pigheaded, headstrong, unyielding, firm, *flexible*

obstruction   barrier, obstacle, snag, hindrance, block

obtain   receive, secure, get, gain, acquire

obvious   clear, plain, apparent, evident, unmistakable, *vague*, *unclear*

obstinate

occasion   chance, opportunity, event

occupation   job, work, business, employment, profession, trade, activity

occur   take place, happen, transpire

ocean   sea, water

95

odd   strange, queer, peculiar, unusual, bizarre, weird, abnormal, curious

odor   scent, smell, fragrance, aroma

offend   insult, displease, wound, disgust, affront

offer   present, propose, suggest

office   1. workplace, headquarters, studio, study

office   2. post, role, position, job

official   formal, authorized, conventional

often   frequently, many times, repeatedly

ogre   fiend, monster, demon

old   elderly, aged, antique, ancient, *young*

omit   exclude, miss, skip, leave out, bar

only   just, merely, simply

ooze   leak, slip out, seep, drip, flow

open   launch, establish, start, begin, initiate, *close*

operate   manage, run, work, conduct, handle, carry on

ooze

opinion   judgment, belief, sentiment, feeling, thought, view, attitude, theory, conception, idea

opponent   foe, enemy, rival, adversary, competitor, *ally*

opportunity   occasion, chance, opening

oppose   disagree, fight, hinder, dispute, argue, resist, contradict, cross, *support*

opposite   different, dissimilar, inverse

optimistic   cheerful, hopeful, positive, carefree, jaunty, *pessimistic*

oral verbal, voiced, spoken, vocalized, sounded

orbit circuit, path, revolution, circle, route

order 1. manner, system, arrangement, mode

order 2. directive, instruction, direction, command

ordinary common, average, usual, normal, everyday, regular, standard, *unusual*

orbit

organize classify, systematize, arrange, set up, categorize, sort, group

origin beginning, inception, source, start

original 1. firsthand, genuine, authentic, *copied*

original 2. new, unusual, novel, fresh, different, unique, *ordinary*

ornament adornment, trimming, decoration, garnish, embellishment

ornery 1. obstinate, pigheaded, stubborn, willful, headstrong, contrary, *flexible*

ornery 2. cross, grouchy, grumpy, cranky, mean, crabby, difficult, *agreeable*, *pleasant*

other different, distinct, extra, fresh, new

ought should, must, need to, have to, be obliged

outcome effect, result, conclusion, consequence, end, upshot, fruit

outdo better, surpass, beat, triumph, outshine

outer exterior, surface, visible, *inner*

outfit furnish, provide, equip, supply, rig

outlaw outcast, exile, criminal, convict

outline plan, sketch, diagram, blueprint, profile

outlaw

outrageous

outlook   point of view, attitude, position, view
outrageous   shocking, insulting, absurd, ridiculous, foolish, ludicrous, extreme, *sensible*, *ordinary*
outsider   outcast, exile
outstanding   distinguished, well-known, extraordinary, important, prominent, conspicuous, noticeable
overcast   cloudy, gloomy, dismal, dark, *clear*
overcome   defeat, overpower, conquer, upset, surmount, *yield*, *surrender*
overlook   neglect, ignore, skip, miss, disregard, pass over
overpass   span, bridge, viaduct
oversight   slip, negligence, error, omission
overthrow   overturn, defeat, overcome, overpower, upset, destroy
owe   be indebted, be obliged, be liable
own   possess, have, hold, maintain

P

package

pace   speed, rate
pack   stuff, load, fill, cram, stow
package   parcel, bundle, box

pact   understanding, contract, agreement, treaty

pad   1. tablet, notebook, ledger

pad   2. cushion, pillow, mat

pageant   exhibition, show, spectacle, parade, display, review, presentation

pail   bucket

pail

pain   hurt, ache, wound, soreness, pang, discomfort

paint   1. color, coat, cover, decorate, adorn

paint   2. illustrate, picture, portray, draw, depict

pair   two, couple, set, twins, mates, duo

pal   friend, buddy, companion, comrade, chum

palace   mansion, castle, villa, chateau

pale   colorless, faint, whitish, pallid, wan, *bright*

pamphlet   brochure, booklet, manual, leaflet, folder

panic   dread, fear, alarm, fright, terror

pants   slacks, trousers

parade   march, procession, pageant, review, display, exhibition, show

paralyze   deaden, numb, disable, cripple

parched   arid, thirsty, dry, dehydrated

pardon   absolve, excuse, forgive, exonerate, acquit, vindicate, *blame*

part   1. segment, portion, piece, section, fraction, share, *whole*

part   2. character, role

participate   enter into, partake, contribute, join, take part in

party

particular critical, finicky, fussy

partner associate, colleague, companion, collaborator

party festivity, celebration, fete

pass 1. succeed, do well, *fail*

pass 2. transfer, hand over, deliver, relay

pass 3. fling, hurl, throw, toss

passage lane, aisle, corridor, opening, channel

passenger rider

paste adhesive, mucilage, glue, cement

pasture field, meadow, grassland, range

patch repair, fix, mend

path track, way, route, trail, road, lane

patience tolerance, endurance, understanding, *impatience*

patriotic nationalistic, loyal, chauvinistic

patrol protect, guard, watch, keep vigil, police

pattern 1. print, picture, design, illustration

pattern 2. role, prototype, model, example

pause stop, wait, recess, break, rest, *continue*

paw handle, touch, feel

pay give, compensate, settle up

peaceful calm, quiet, serene, still, harmonious, *hectic*

peak summit, pinnacle, top, crest, tip, crown, *base*

pebble rock, stone, chip

peculiar unusual, weird, strange, odd, queer, bizarre, *normal*, *ordinary*

peddle   vend, hawk, sell
pedestrian   walker
peek   peer, glance, glimpse, look
peer   peep, peek, look, glimpse, gaze
penalty   fine, punishment, tax
penetrate   pierce, enter, puncture
penmanship   script, handwriting
pennant   streamer, banner, flag, standard

pennant

pep   energy, vigor, vitality, spirit, vim
perfect   flawless, faultless, excellent, ideal, right,
  imperfect, *defective*
perform   carry out, do, accomplish, execute, achieve,
  transact
perfume   odor, fragrance, aroma, scent
perhaps   possibly, conceivably, maybe
period   span, interval, time, era

perish   succumb, expire, die, decease, vanish,
  disappear
permanent   unchanging, lasting, steady, constant,
  stable, *temporary*

pep

permit   let, allow, consent, admit
person   human, individual, somebody, someone
personal   individual, private, special, specific,
  particular
personality   character, temperament, identity,
  individuality
perspire   sweat

pet

phantom

persuade convince, convert, win over, reach, induce

pessimistic gloomy, unhappy, negative, hopeless, despairing, downhearted, cynical, *optimistic*

pest nuisance, annoyance, bother, disturbance

pester disturb, annoy, nag, tease, bother, harass, molest

pet 1. choice, favorite, dear one

pet 2. caress, stroke, fondle, pat

petite small, little, tiny, slight, miniature, delicate, dainty, *big*

petrified 1. terrified, scared, frightened, appalled, shocked, horrified, stunned, paralyzed

petrified 2. stonelike, solidified, hardened, frozen

petty minor, trivial, small, unimportant, meaningless, puny, *important*

phantom spirit, ghost, spook, fantasy, vision, wraith, illusion, specter

pharmacist druggist, chemist

photograph picture, snapshot

phrase clause, part, section, fragment, passage

physical corporeal, bodily, carnal

physician doctor, medic

pick select, choose, opt, elect, gather, harvest

picture representation, drawing, illustration, design

piece section, part, segment, portion, chunk, bit, hunk, share, division

pier wharf, dock

pierce break through, probe, puncture, penetrate, stab

pile mound, stack, heap, collection, load, batch

pill drug, medication, medicine

pillow cushion, bolster, headrest

pin clasp, fasten, attach, clip, hook

pioneer colonist, forerunner, settler, leader

piracy stealing, swiping, pillaging, plundering, thievery

pistol revolver, gun, firearm

pitch throw, fling, toss, cast, hurl, heave, sling

pity compassion, mercy, sympathy, empathy, regard

place lay, set, put, deposit, arrange, compose, station

plain 1. understandable, simple, clear, distinct, unmistakable, obvious, evident, apparent, *complicated*

plain 2. homely, unattractive, dull, *pretty*

plan propose, aim, intend, project, figure

plastic changeable, variable, mobile, fluid, flexible, pliant

plate dish, bowl, crockery, china

play 1. frolic, romp

play 2. perform, present

playful lively, frisky, spirited, gay, impish, sportive, frolicsome, animated, mischievous, vivacious

plead beg, appeal, petition, ask, request

playful

pleasant   desirable, agreeable, likable, pleasing, cheerful, charming, happy, delightful, appealing, genial, satisfying, *unpleasant*

pledge   oath, vow, promise, agreement, pact, treaty, commitment

plenty   enough, ample, sufficient, a lot, adequate, abundant, lavish, *insufficient*

plot   concoct, devise, scheme, plan, maneuver, conspire

plug   clog, jam, stop, block, obstruct, congest, stuff, *unplug, open, clear*

plump   stout, chubby, stocky, heavy, fat, chunky, pudgy, tubby, obese, fleshy, corpulent, *thin*

plump

plunge   plummet, fall, dive, drop

poetry   verse, rhyme, lyric, ode

point   indicate, show, direct, aim

pointless   meaningless, aimless, purposeless

poised   composed, collected, balanced, confident, assured

poisonous   deadly, venomous, toxic, noxious

poke   thrust, ram, jab, push, goad, spur, shove

pole   bar, rod, shaft, post, beam, stick

police   watch, guard, shield, patrol, defend, secure

poisonous

policy   plan, program, procedure, course, principles, platform

polish   buff, shine, wax, rub, glaze, smooth

polite   courteous, well-mannered, gracious, respectful, civil, tactful, *impolite, rude*

political   social, issue-oriented

politician   candidate, officer, official, office-holder, leader

poll   survey, canvass, questionnaire, vote, referendum

polluted   impure, foul, contaminated, infected, dirty, poisoned, tainted, defiled, *pure, clean*

pond   pool, lake, lagoon

poor   impoverished, penniless, destitute, needy, *rich*

popular   1. usual, regular, common, customary, ordinary, conventional, *unusual*

popular   2. well-liked, admired, cherished, favorite, beloved, adored, *unpopular, disliked*

portable   transferable, mobile, movable, conveyable

portion   section, part, piece, segment, division, share, fraction

popular

portrait   picture, representation, depiction, illustration, description

pose   posture, position, bearing, carriage, pretense

position   1. location, spot, place, situation

position   2. function, role, job, office, post

positive   definite, certain, sure, absolute, optimistic, *unsure, negative*

possessions   property, goods, belongings

possible   feasible, probable, likely, conceivable, imaginable, *impossible*

post 1. notify, announce, list, inform

post 2. duty, position, job, office, assignment

postpone delay, put off, procrastinate, stall, defer, suspend

posture position, carriage, bearing

pounce jump, swoop, spring, hop, bound, hurdle, vault, plunge, dive, leap

pound hit, strike, beat, rap, knock, punch, pummel, bang

pour drain, flow, spew, spill, stream

poverty impoverishment, destitution, neediness, deprivation

power 1. force, might, strength, energy, vigor, potency

power 2. influence, control, authority, command, mastery, domination

practical useful, usable, efficient, effective

practically nearly, almost, approximately, essentially

practice train, exercise, drill, rehearse, repeat

praise flatter, extol, compliment, glorify

pray appeal, plead, beg, petition, entreat, implore, beseech

precious 1. expensive, valuable, priceless, costly, *cheap*

precious 2. loved, special, cherished, adored

precipitation rain, moisture, snow, hail, sleet

praise

precise   exact, definite, specific, accurate, *approximate*

predicament   dilemma, quandary, mess, plight, problem

predict   foresee, foretell, forecast, prophesy

prefer   favor, choose, like

prejudiced   biased, partial, intolerant, *neutral*, *fair*

I PREDICT... YOU WILL WIN THE RACE!

predict

prepare   get ready, concoct, arrange, fix, set up

present   offering, gift, donation, contribution

preserve   save, keep, conserve, hoard, maintain, protect, guard, defend, shelter, screen, sustain, *destroy*, *neglect*

press   1. force, push, clasp, squeeze, tighten

press   2. urge, insist, coax, goad, prod, stress

press   3. smooth, iron

pretend   make believe, bluff, fake, act, sham, feign

pretty   good-looking, lovely, attractive, cute, *unattractive*, *homely*

ICE COLD SODA

BOY AM I THIRSTY!

press

prevent   keep from, block, stop, hinder, deter, bar, obstruct, *allow*

previous   prior, earlier, former, onetime, preceding

price   cost, amount, rate, value, charge, worth

pride   self-esteem, self-respect, dignity, arrogance, vanity

primary   first, major, chief, main, principal, leading, essential, basic

primitive   1. ancient, prehistoric, original, *modern*

primitive 2. barbaric, crude, uncivilized, prehistoric, *sophisticated*

principal main, chief, dominant, leading, important

principle belief, doctrine, law, rule, precept

print issue, put out, publish, publicize

prison penitentiary, jail, lockup, reformatory

private personal, intimate, secret, hidden, secluded, withdrawn

privilege right, license, advantage, liberty

prize award, treasure, reward

probable likely, liable, apt, presumable, *improbable*

probe examine, scrutinize, investigate, search, explore

problem mystery, puzzle, question, issue

procedure policy, practice, rule, plan, custom, way, method, manner, means

proceed advance, progress, go ahead, go forward

process operation, procedure, course, step, act, way, manner, means, mode

produce create, make, manufacture

profession occupation, career, job, work, calling, vocation

profit gain, benefit, advantage, earnings, returns, proceeds

program agenda, plan, list, schedule, roster, calendar

progress go forward, advance, proceed, improve

WOW!

prize

prohibit   ban, bar, forbid, prevent, refuse, obstruct, *allow*

project   venture, enterprise, undertaking, plan, scheme

promise   pledge, guarantee, vow, swear, agree, commit

promising   encouraging, hopeful, probable, favorable, likely

prompt   1. on time, ready, punctual, *late*

prompt   2. cue, remind, coach, push, inspire

proof   evidence, demonstration, verification, identification

proper   right, correct, suitable, appropriate, decent, fitting, moral, *improper*, *wrong*

property   belongings, holdings, possessions, goods

proportion   ratio, measure, amount, balance, share, percentage

prosperous

prosperous   rich, wealthy, successful, affluent, comfortable, well-to-do, well-off, thriving

protect   shield, safeguard, defend, cover, support, care for

protest   challenge, complain, object, differ

proud   gratified, pleased, vain, egotistical, arrogant, *humble*

prove   verify, demonstrate, document, confirm, show, certify

provide   furnish, give, supply, avail

proud

pry

pull

province   division, department, sphere, territory, region, zone, principality

provoke   tease, taunt, annoy, bother, disturb, anger, irritate, antagonize, vex, exasperate

pry   1. snoop, mix, meddle, peek, peer

pry   2. wrench, jimmy, loosen

public   people, populace, society, population, persons

publicity   advertisements, notice, exposure

publish   issue, print, publicize

puddle   pool, pond

pull   tow, tug, drag, draw, haul, yank, attract, *push*

pulse   throb, heartbeat, palpitation

punch   strike, beat, pound, hit, batter, knock, slug, wallop, slam, pummel

punctual   on time, prompt, ready, speedy, immediate, quick, *late*

puncture   penetrate, stab, pierce, perforate

punish   chastise, correct, discipline, penalize

pupil   student, scholar, schoolchild

purchase   buy, shop, acquire, *sell*

pure   genuine, sacred, cleansed, clear, unadulterated

purify   clean, cleanse, refine, filter, clarify, clear, *pollute*, *soil*

purpose   object, aim, goal, intention, target, design

pursue   chase, follow, seek, shadow, trail, quest, hunt

110

push   shove, thrust, press, drive, force, propel, nudge, *pull*

put   lay, place, deposit, set, arrange, *remove*

puzzle   problem, enigma, mystery, dilemma, confusion, quandary, bewilderment

Q

quack   fake, phony, impostor, pretender

quaint   curious, charming, old-fashioned

quake   tremble, shake, quiver, vibrate, shiver, shudder

qualified   suited, capable, competent, fit, efficient, able, eligible, *unqualified*, *unfit*

quality   characteristic, feature, trait, nature, constitution

quantity   sum, amount, measure, number, portion, volume, mass, multitude

quarrel   squabble, fight, bicker, disagree, argue, dispute

queer   strange, odd, unusual, abnormal, peculiar, curious

quench   slake, satisfy, extinguish, suppress, put out, squelch

quarrel

question

question   interrogate, inquire, ask, query, demand, *answer*

quick   1. speedy, hasty, rapid, fast, swift, *slow*

quick   2. alert, bright, keen, sharp, attentive, *slow, dull*

quiet   hushed, still, silent, peaceful, *noisy*

quirk   oddity, feature, trait

quit   cease, stop, give up, conclude, halt, finish, discontinue, abandon, *continue*

quiver

quiver   shiver, tremble, shake, vibrate, quaver

quiz   examination, test, interrogation

quote   cite, echo, repeat, refer to

R

race   1. speed, run, dash, rush, sprint, hurry, tear, dart, scoot

race   2. ancestry, nationality, people, nation

rack   framework, shelf

racket   1. commotion, noise, disturbance, din, hubbub, uproar, clamor, tumult

racket   2. swindle, fraud, hustle

rage

rage 1. frenzy, violence, anger, ire, furor, passion, mania

rage 2. trend, fad, fashion, style

ragged worn, torn, frayed, shabby, shoddy

raid assault, invade, attack, plunder, loot

raise 1. hoist, elevate, lift, boost, erect

raise 2. produce, bring up, rear

rake gather, collect

rank position, class, grade, status

rap knock, tap, hammer, bang

rapid speedy, hasty, swift, fast, quick, fleet, rushed

rare uncommon, scarce, precious, unusual, unique, *common*

rate evaluate, grade, appraise, rank, measure, compare

raw uncooked, *cooked*

ray gleam, beam, light, stream

reach arrive at, approach, land

react answer, respond

ready set, prepared, fit

real true, genuine, actual, authentic, legitimate, bona fide, *fake*

realize conceive, comprehend, understand, grasp, appreciate

rear 1. hind, back, posterior, *front*

rear 2. produce, raise, bring up, create, foster

rearrange reorder, classify, categorize

reason excuse, cause, explanation, motive, basis, justification, sense

reasonable sensible, fair, sound, logical, just, sane, rational, realistic, practical, *unreasonable, unfair*

reassure comfort, console, soothe, calm, quiet

rebel defy, disobey, revolt, riot, resist, *obey*

recall recollect, remember, reminisce, review, *forget*

receive get, take in, obtain, gain, admit, accept, *give*

recent current, up-to-date, new, modern, late, contemporary, *past, old*

recess rest, stop, pause, break

recipe formula, directions, instructions, prescription

recite narrate, recount, relate, tell, repeat, review, rehearse

reckless heedless, wild, careless, rash, thoughtless, impetuous, sloppy, hasty, inconsiderate, *thoughtful*

recognize acknowledge, know

reckless

recommend suggest, advocate, advise, counsel

record list, write, log, enter, inscribe

recover 1. regain, rescue, get back, reclaim, retrieve, *lose*

recover 2. improve, rally, heal, get better, recuperate, revive, *decline*

recreation amusement, play, pleasure, entertainment, enjoyment, fun, pastime, diversion

reduce lessen, lower, shrink, cut, diminish, decrease, moderate, *increase*

referee

refer   direct, point, send, recommend, allude

referee   umpire, judge, mediator

reflect   1. mirror, echo

reflect   2. deliberate, ponder, study, muse, mull over, contemplate, meditate

reform   revise, change, improve, convert

refrigerate   chill, cool, ice

refund   reimburse, repay

1. refuse   decline, reject, rebuff

2. refuse   waste, garbage, rubbish, trash, litter

regal   majestic, royal, dignified, noble, stately, grand

region   location, area, district, territory, vicinity, zone, place, space

register   enlist, sign up, enroll, enter, join

regular   ordinary, common, normal, familiar, usual, everyday, normal, typical, *unusual*

regal

regulate   1. manage, govern, handle, direct, rule, control, command, run

regulate   2. adjust, remedy, rectify, correct

rehearse   practice, drill, exercise, repeat, prepare, train

reign   rule, prevail

reject   cast off, refuse, expel, discard, decline, eliminate, exclude, bar

relate   recount, tell, narrate, recite, report, repeat, describe, state

related   associated, connected, linked, akin, affiliated

relationship involvement, connection, link, influence

relative contingent, dependent

relax unwind, rest, release

release let go, free, dismiss, discharge, expel, *keep,*
hold

reliable trustworthy, faithful, dependable, steadfast,
loyal, true, devoted, safe, sure, stable, *unreliable*

relief 1. assistance, aid, help

relief 2. comfort, alleviation, ease, freedom

relief 3. substitution, change, alternate, replacement

religious devout, pious, observant

rely trust, count, depend, confide

remain persist, continue, stay, last, endure

remark comment, observation, statement

remarkable noteworthy, incredible, unusual, special,
striking, exceptional, memorable, wonderful,
marvelous, rare, *ordinary*

remarkable

remedy treatment, cure, relief, solution

remember recollect, recall, reminisce, review,
recognize, *forget*

remind prompt, suggest

remove eliminate, take away, withdraw, discard,
expel, oust, *leave, retain*

rent hire, let, lease, charter

repair fix, mend, patch, adjust, service, restore,
overhaul, *break*

repeat reiterate, echo, duplicate

replace replenish, refill, restore

reply response, answer, retort, reaction

report describe, tell, repeat, relate, narrate, recount

represent 1. portray, depict, illustrate, symbolize, characterize, express, describe

represent 2. exhibit, show, demonstrate, display, manifest, present, reveal, disclose

reputation honor, repute, character, name, fame, distinction

request ask for, requisition, apply for

require want, lack, need, demand

rescue salvage, save, redeem, recover, retrieve, free

rescue

research inquiry, investigation, exploration, probe

resemblance similarity, likeness, sameness

resentment displeasure, irritation, vexation, bitterness, indignation

reserve hold, save, keep, store, put aside

resign quit, leave, give up, yield

resist oppose, withstand, counteract

respect value, appreciate, admire, esteem, honor, revere

respond answer, reply, retort, react

responsible dependable, reliable, trustworthy, answerable, liable, faithful, loyal, *irresponsible*

rest 1. unwind, relax, pause, recover

rest 2. balance, remains, leftovers, remainder

rest

restless   edgy, impatient, fidgety, uneasy, disturbed, troubled, *calm*, *composed*

restore   reinstate, renovate, repair, renew, mend

restrain   control, check, suppress, arrest, inhibit, curb, smother, stifle, impede, limit, restrict, confine

restriction   restraint, limitation, constraint

result   consequence, outcome, effect, end, upshot, fruit

retire   quit, leave, resign, abdicate

retreat   withdraw, retire, reverse

return   1. revisit, go back, revert, *leave*

return   2. give back, reimburse, repay

reunion   gathering, get-together, assembly, meeting

reveal   expose, show, display, uncover, disclose, *hide*

reveal

revenge   retaliate, avenge

reverse   switch, revert, regress, return, overturn, go back

review   learn, remember, recall, study

revive   resuscitate, refresh, restore, bring back

revolution   1. uprising, revolt, rebellion, overthrow

revolution   2. orbit, circle, cycle

reward   prize, award, payment, compensation, remuneration

rhythm   tempo, beat, swing, meter

rich   well-off, well-to-do, affluent, comfortable, wealthy, prosperous, *poor*

THANK YOU ... FOR FINDING MY NECKLACE!

reward

ridiculous   silly, foolish, outrageous, stupid, unbelievable, absurd, ludicrous

right   accurate, correct, fitting, suitable, good, valid, proper, true, sound, *wrong*

rigid   firm, stiff, hard, unbending, unyielding, *flexible*, *soft*

rim   border, edge, fringe, frame, margin

ring   1. circle, band

ring   2. sound, peal, toll, chime, tinkle

riot   uprising, revolt, mutiny, rebellion, brawl

rip   tear, slit, slash, split, cut, break

ripe   mature, ready, full-grown, developed, *unripe*, *green*

rise   1. get up, stand, *sit*

rise   2. advance, ascend, mount, *descend*

rise   3. increase, grow, gain, *decrease*, *fall*

risk   gamble, chance, hazard, venture, endanger, imperil

river   stream, current, rivulet, creek, waterway

road   way, route, path, street, lane, thoroughfare

roam   meander, drift, wander, rove, ramble, stray

roar   thunder, clamor, boom

rob   burglarize, loot, steal, sack, pillage

role   character, part, position, function

room   space, scope, leeway, latitude

root   cause, source, origin

rot   decay, spoil, disintegrate

ring

rotate

rotate turn, spin, swivel, pivot, gyrate, orbit

rough 1. coarse, bumpy, jagged, uneven, broken, choppy, irregular, *smooth*

rough 2. rowdy, harsh, crude, brusque, tough, curt, *gentle*

round circular, rotund, spherical, globular

route path, course, rounds, itinerary

routine system, habit, method, arrangement, order, custom, practice, patterns

rove wander, roam, stray, drift, ramble, meander

row 1. series, line, string, column, sequence

row 2. paddle, scull

rowdy disorderly, misbehaving, rough, boisterous, disobedient, naughty, *well-behaved*

royal regal, noble, stately, majestic, dignified, grand

rub massage, stroke, buff, scour

rubbish trash, garbage, waste, junk, scrap, refuse, litter

rude discourteous, ungracious, disrespectful, impolite, uncivil, insolent, ill-mannered, vulgar, boorish, *polite*

rug carpet, covering, mat

ruin wreck, destroy, mar, spoil, ravage, demolish, devastate

rule 1. command, control, govern, manage, regulate, lead, head

rule 2. law, regulation

ruler

ruler   king, queen, monarch, emperor, empress, dictator, head

rumor   gossip, talk, chatter

run   1. hasten, hurry, jog, sprint, dash, race

run   2. regulate, control, govern, manage, command, lead, head, direct, rule, supervise

run   3. work, operate, use

run   4. pour, gush, flow, stream, spurt

run   5. electioneer, campaign, seek office

rush   dash, hasten, hurry, speed, hustle, accelerate

rusty   corroded, eroded, decaying

ruthless   heartless, cruel, brutal, merciless, mean, savage, *merciful*

S

sacred   spiritual, holy, religious, sacrosanct

sacrifice   relinquish, surrender, yield, forfeit, release

sad   downhearted, depressed, unhappy, glum, blue, forlorn, melancholy, gloomy, sorrowful

safe   protected, guarded, secure, defended, *dangerous*

sag   droop, trail, drag, hang

salary   compensation, wages, pay, earnings

sample   try, test, experiment, taste

sand   file, smooth, scrape, rub, grind, buff

sane   sensible, rational, reasonable, sound, logical

sanitary   hygienic, clean, pure, sterile, *unsanitary,*
   dirty

sap   drain, weaken, debilitate

sarcastic   bitter, cutting, stinging, sharp, insulting

satisfied   gratified, content, pleased, fulfilled,
   displeased

save   1. conserve, keep, preserve, accumulate, store,
   economize, *discard, spend*

save   2. rescue, retrieve, salvage, recover, redeem

say   declare, tell, speak, exclaim, state, remark,
   express, utter, mention, comment, proclaim

scald   scorch, sear, burn

scale   climb, mount

scar   wound, blemish, mark, bruise, mar

scarce   scanty, rare, meager, sparse, *plentiful*

scare   startle, frighten, shock, unnerve, alarm, upset,
   terrify, *soothe, calm*

scatter   distribute, strew, disperse, spread, *gather*

scene   sight, view, picture, setting, panorama, vista

scent   smell, odor, fragrance, aroma

schedule   agenda, plan, list, program, line-up, slate,
   calendar

scheme   plan, plot, intrigue, conspiracy

scold   reprove, chastise, admonish, reprimand, chide

scare

scorch

scorch singe, burn, char, sear, blacken, parch

score tally, sum, count, total, figure

scoundrel scamp, devil, imp, rascal, rogue, villain

scour clean, scrub, wash, wipe

scout search, explore, seek, hunt

scramble jumble, combine, mix, blend, stir, *separate*

scrap 1. shred, speck, small amount, fragment, piece

scrap 2. junk, litter, trash, rubbish, garbage, waste, debris

scrape grate, rub

scoundrel

scratch scar, scrape, cut, mark, graze, score

scream shout, cry, howl, yell, shriek, wail, screech, yelp

screech squeak, shriek, yell, howl, cry, shout, wail, squeal, yowl

screen net, veil, shade, guard, shield

screw fasten, rotate, tighten, turn, twist

scribble write, scratch, scrawl

script penmanship, writing, handwriting

scrub clean, scour, wash, rub, wipe, buff

sculpture shape, form, carve, model, mold, chisel

seal 1. secure, fasten, close, bind, shut, *open*

seal 2. engraving, sign, mark, stamp

seal 3. sea lion

sear singe, burn, scorch, blacken, char

search seek, hunt, scout, explore, investigate, probe

season spice, flavor

secret

selfish

secret   hidden, private, secluded, intimate

section   segment, portion, part, share, fragment, piece

secure   guarded, protected, safe, sound, firm, stable, *insecure, unsafe*

seek   hunt, scout, search, explore

seem   appear, look

seep   trickle, leak, ooze, drip

segment   piece, division, portion, part, section, fraction

seize   grasp, grab, clutch, snatch, clasp, *release*

seldom   infrequently, hardly, rarely, *frequently, often*

select   pick, choose, opt

self-conscious   bashful, timid, shy, coy, embarrassed, *confident*

selfish   egotistical, greedy, self-centered, possessive, stingy, *generous, openhanded*

sell   vend, market, peddle, *buy*

send   transmit, relay, forward, dispatch, convey, *receive*

sensational   wonderful, marvelous, divine, extraordinary, spectacular, thrilling, exciting, great, glorious, grand, splendid, superb, magnificent, *dull, ordinary*

sense   1. feel, perceive, realize, discern

sense   2. intelligence, judgment, mentality

senseless   silly, foolish, inane, idiotic, dumb, stupid, *sensible*

sensible   logical, reasonable, realistic, practical, intelligent, rational, wise, understanding, *foolish*

sensitive   tender, vulnerable

separate   split, divide, sort, part, break up, isolate, *unite*, *join*

sequel   follow-up, continuation, continuance

series   group, sequence

serious   1. grave, solemn, grim, somber, pensive, *carefree*, *gay*

serious   2. significant, meaningful, important, major, weighty, *trivial*, *unimportant*

sermon   talk, lecture, discourse

serpent   viper, snake

servant   maid, butler, attendant

serve   help, assist, aid, oblige

service   assistance, employment, aid, duty

set   1. put down, place, arrange, deposit, position

set   2. adjust, fix, regulate

settle   1. resolve, decide, reconcile, mend, patch up, determine

settle   2. live, inhabit, reside, occupy, locate

several   various, numerous, many, some, a lot, *few*

severe   cruel, harsh, rough, hard, extreme, tough, strict, *mild*

sew   stitch, hem, baste

shabby   worn, torn, ragged, seedy, shoddy, frayed

shack   shanty, cabin, hut, shed

shack

shade shadow, coolness, shelter, darkness

shadow darkness, gloom, shade, covering, disguise

shake quake, quiver, shudder, tremble, vibrate

shallow featherbrained, simple, empty, vacant, superficial, *deep, profound*

shameful dishonorable, disgraceful, awful, scandalous, humiliating

shampoo lather, soap, wash

shape fashion, make, develop, form, construct, create, design, mold, sculpt

share split, divide, apportion, distribute, allot

sharp 1. angular, cutting, pointy, *dull*

sharp 2. clever, bright, quick, alert, keen, shrewd, quick-witted, brainy, *stupid, dull*

shatter fracture, break, crush, crack, smash, split, fragment, destroy

sharp

shelter 1. quarters, housing

shelter 2. refuge, cover, protection, safeguard, harbor

shield defend, protect, cover, safeguard, cloak, screen

shift switch, transfer, alter, change, substitute

shine gleam, glow, glimmer, sparkle, beam, twinkle, glisten

shiver shudder, quiver, shake, tremble, quake

shock stun, surprise, startle, jolt, jar

shoot discharge, fire

shop purchase, buy

shore beach, coast, waterfront, harbor

short

short 1. tiny, small, little, puny, *tall*

short 2. concise, brief, terse, succinct, *long*

shortage need, want, lack, deprivation, deficiency, absence, *abundance*

shout howl, yell, scream, call, cry, bawl

shove bump, push, nudge

show 1. indicate, illustrate, demonstrate, clarify, explain, reveal

show 2. presentation, performance, exhibit, production, play, display

shower rainstorm, downpour, sprinkling, drizzle

shrewd keen, clever, bright, sharp, knowing, crafty, alert, foxy, canny, quick-witted, sly, *dull, slow naive*

shriek howl, yell, scream, shout, cry, wail, screech, call

shrink shrivel, become smaller, reduce, wither, condense, *expand, grow*

shrug toss off, shake off

shudder shiver, quiver, quake, tremble, shake

shuffle jumble, scramble, mix, rearrange

shut close, lock, fasten, seal, *open*

shy modest, timid, bashful, demure, coy, *bold aggressive*

sick ailing, infirm, ill, invalid, *healthy*

sigh grieve, moan, lament, mourn, cry

sight scene, view, panorama, vista, spectacle, picture

sick

sign   1. write, endorse, mark, seal

sign   2. motion, signal, wave, gesture, indication

signature   autograph, endorsement

silent   quiet, hushed, still, mute, noiseless, *noisy*

silly   foolish, trivial, inane, senseless, *sensible*

similar   like, same, resembling, alike, related

simmer   bubble, boil, cook, seethe

simple   1. clear, easy, straightforward, uncomplicated, *difficult*

silly

simple   2. ordinary, plain, common

sin   offense, wrongdoing, evil, crime

sincere   truthful, honest, unaffected, genuine, authentic, *phony*

sing   chant, croon, vocalize, hum, serenade

singe   scorch, char, sear, burn, blacken

singer   vocalist

single   alone, sole, unique

site   location, place, spot, area, position, region

situation   condition, case, terms, circumstance

size   girth, width, length, proportion, dimensions, scope, extent

skillful   clever, expert, handy, adept, apt, capable, able, *unskillful, awkward*

singer

skimpy   spare, scanty, sparse, meager, *generous*

skinny   lean, thin, slim, scrawny, lanky, gaunt, bony, *fat*

128

skip   omit, leave out, miss, pass over, jump over, exclude, *include*

slam   bang, shut, close

slant   incline, tilt, slope, tip, lean

slap   strike, smack, hit, bang

slash   sever, cut, slit, wound, gash

slavery   bondage, captivity, servitude, *freedom*

slay   slaughter, murder, kill, assassinate, exterminate, destroy, butcher

sleep   slumber, nap, doze, drowse, snooze

slice   slit, carve, cut, slash

slide   skid, glide, skim, slip

slim   slender, svelte, skinny, thin

sling   splint, bandage, support

slip   1. skid, glide, fall, slide

slip   2. oversight, blunder, error, mistake

slit   split, cut, slash, tear, gash

slope   tilt, incline, slant, lean

sloppy   untidy, messy, careless, dirty, slovenly, *neat*

slow   1. slack, tardy, leisurely, poky, sluggish, *fast*

slow   2. stupid, dumb, dull, dim-witted, *bright*

slug   punch, poke, hit, belt, smack

sly   cunning, sneaky, knowing, crafty, shrewd, shifty, underhanded

smack   hit, crack, slap, whack, swat, wallop

small   slight, tiny, little, puny, miniature, *big*

small

smart

smile

smart   1. bright, intelligent, clever, wise, alert, brilliant, quick, genius, *stupid*

smart   2. hurt, ache, pain, sting

smash   demolish, crush, break, destroy, split, devastate, shatter, crack

smear   1. soil, smudge, tarnish, stain, spot

smear   2. coat, spread, dab, rub

smell   aroma, odor, scent, fragrance

smile   grin, beam, smirk, *frown*

smog   cloudiness, haziness, fog, pollution

smoke   smoulder, fume, reek, steam, puff, inhale

smooth   glossy, slick, sleek, polished, level, even, *rough*

snake   viper, serpent

snarl   growl, grumble

snatch   grasp, seize, grab, clutch, hook, snare, trap

sneak   lurk, slink, steal, creep, prowl

snooze   drowse, nap, sleep, drop off, doze

snug   comfortable, secure, cozy, sheltered, homelike

soak   drench, wet, saturate, steep, *dry*

soap   lather, shampoo

sob   bawl, wail, cry, weep

sober   serious, sensible, moderate, calm, reasonable

sociable   friendly, amiable, cordial, congenial, gregarious

social   political, societal

society group, organization, association, company, world, milieu

sofa divan, couch, loveseat

soft fluffy, flexible, delicate, tender, yielding, pliable, *hard*

soggy moist, wet, damp, watery, humid, *dry*

soil 1. smudge, stain, spot, dirty, smear

soil 2. dirt, land, earth, ground

soldier warrior, recruit, enlistee, draftee

solemn grave, serious, sad, gloomy, grim, somber, glum, dismal, *cheerful*

solid rigid, firm, hard, strong, sturdy, inflexible, immovable, unchanging, *flimsy*, *soft*

solo alone, unaccompanied, single, solitary

solution outcome, finding, answer, result, explanation

solve figure out, explain, answer, discover, work out, decode, decipher

song melody, tune, lyric, ditty

soon presently, quickly, directly, promptly, shortly

soothe comfort, calm, quiet, pacify, ease, relieve

sore aching, tender, painful, smarting, irritated

sorrow grief, suffering, trouble, sadness, misfortune, anguish, misery, depression, *joy*

sorry regretful, apologetic, remorseful

sort organize, arrange, group, classify, categorize, divide

sound tone, strain, noise

sore

sour   tart, acid, bitter, lemony

source   origin, beginning, wellspring

souvenir   keepsake, memento, token, relic, remembrance

space   extent, expanse, room, measure, dimension, area

spacious   roomy, vast, expansive, broad, *cramped*

spar   fight, box

spare   extra, surplus, remainder, balance, leftover, excess

sparkle   glimmer, shine, flash, glisten, glitter, twinkle, beam

speak   talk, proclaim, comment, announce

special   notable, unusual, outstanding, remarkable, exceptional, extraordinary, noteworthy, *ordinary*

specific   definite, precise, fixed, special

spectacular   marvelous, sensational, dramatic, glorious, wonderful, great, extraordinary, superb, magnificent, grand, thrilling, exciting, splendid, *dull, ordinary*

speech   lecture, reading, sermon, talk, oration

speedy   swift, rapid, fast, fleet, hasty, quick, *slow*

spend   pay out, lay out, use, consume, *save*

spice   flavor, season

spill   overflow, cascade, flood, pour, run over, brim over

spin   twirl, swirl, turn, pivot, rotate

sparkle

spirit bravery, spunk, nerve, courage

spiteful nasty, malicious, mean, vindictive

splendid magnificent, great, glorious, grand, superb, wonderful, majestic, fabulous, sensational, divine, excellent, fine

split fracture, crack, fragment, separate, break, divide

spoil 1. botch, harm, damage, mar, hurt, ruin, destroy, impair, upset

spoil 2. decay, rot

sponsor promoter, underwriter, supporter, backer

spook wraith, spirit, ghost, phantom

sport fun, game, play, contest, amusement

spot

spot 1. stain, dirty, soil, smear, smudge, blot

spot 2. sight, spy, pick out, identify, recognize, discern, distinguish

spray splash, sprinkle, splatter

spread 1. extend, sprawl, unfold, stretch out

spread 2. disperse, scatter, distribute

spry sprightly, active, lively, energetic, agile, spirited, nimble, *sluggish*

squad team, crew, gang, group

squander misspend, throw away, waste, *save*

spray

squash mash, crush, destroy, squeeze, demolish

squeeze pinch, embrace, crush, press

squirt splash, spurt, spout, spray, jet, gush

stab puncture, penetrate, pierce, perforate, break through

stack load, pile, mound, heap

stage rostrum, podium, platform, proscenium

stain spot, smear, dirty, mark, smudge, soil, discolor

stale spoiled, old, dull, *fresh*

stall postpone, put off, delay, procrastinate

stammer stutter, hesitate, falter

stamp 1. mark, engraving, seal, label

stamp 2. stomp, bang, pound, kick

stampede panic, flight, rush

stand 1. get up, rise, arise

stand 2. remain, continue, stay

stand 3. endure, bear, suffer, tolerate

stand 4. pedestal, base

stand 5. kiosk, booth

standard 1. usual, normal, typical, everyday, common

standard 2. model, rule, pattern, criterion, ideal

standard 3. flag, pennant, symbol, colors

stanza measure, verse, chorus

staple 1. join, connect, fasten, attach

staple 2. chief, major, principal, established, regular

staple 3. product, commodity, raw material

star 1. headliner, main attraction, lead

star 2. heavenly body

stare gawk, look, glare, gape, gaze

star

start   begin, launch, commence, set out, *end*

startle   stun, surprise, shock, upset, frighten, unnerve

starvation   deprivation, famine, hunger

startle

state   announce, proclaim, declare, tell, say, report, relate, express

statement   report, account, declaration, notice, announcement

station   depot, stop

stationary   immovable, firm, fixed, rigid, *movable*

stationery   writing paper

statue   sculpture, figure, form

stay   stand, continue, remain, endure, persist

steady   constant, regular, unchanging, continuous, *changing*

steal   burglarize, take, rob, plunder

steam   gas, vapor, haze, smoke, mist

statue

steer   direct, handle, drive, lead, conduct, manage, run, command, head

step   tread, walk, pace

sterilize   disinfect, sanitize, clean, decontaminate

stern   harsh, exacting, austere, strict, rough, hard, tough, severe, firm, *easygoing*, *lenient*

stick   cling, adhere, attach, fasten

stiff   hard, firm, rigid, unbending, inflexible, immovable, *soft*

still   calm, quiet, serene, peaceful, tranquil, motionless, *noisy*

135

sting

storm

sting   wound, ache, prick, pang

stingy   selfish, miserly, tight, cheap, close-fisted, *generous*

stink   odor, stench, smell, aroma

stir   blend, mix, scramble, combine, jumble, merge

stock   reserve, collection, inventory, supply, store

stomach   abdomen, belly, paunch

stone   pebble, rock

stool   chair, seat

stop   halt, end, quit, cease, discontinue, terminate, conclude, *start*

store   1. save, conserve, collect, keep, stock

store   2. market, shop, stand, kiosk

storm   tempest, tornado, hurricane, thunderstorm, gale, hailstorm

story   fable, narrative, account, tale, fairy tale

stout   chunky, tubby, plump, husky, chubby, fat, stocky, *thin*

straight   direct, unswerving, unbent

strange   unusual, odd, weird, bizarre, queer, peculiar, extraordinary, *ordinary*

stranger   alien, outsider, foreigner

strangle   suffocate, smother, choke

stray   drift, wander, rove, roam, meander

stream   brook, creek, river, rivulet

street   road, lane, thoroughfare, avenue, path

strength   force, energy, power, might, vitality, vigor, *weakness*

stress   force, strain, pressure, tension, anxiety

stretch   spread, expand, extend, reach

strict   tough, harsh, severe, austere, stern, exact, firm, demanding, *lenient*

strike   slap, bat, hit, swat, slug, smack, belt, knock

strip   bare, uncover, peel, remove, denude, *cover*

stroke   massage, caress, pet, rub, pat, fondle

stroll   saunter, walk, promenade, strut, amble

strong   hardy, sturdy, powerful, mighty, tough, rugged, vital, healthy, muscular, robust, capable, *weak*

structure   form, figure, configuration, shape

struggle   fight, battle, combat, dispute, feud, conflict

stubborn   pigheaded, ornery, insistent, obstinate, firm, willful, headstrong, *flexible*

student   pupil, learner

study   examine, peruse, scrutinize, probe

stuff   cram, load, fill, pack, jam, *empty*

stumble   tumble, stagger, trip, falter, flounder

stun   startle, shock, unnerve, jolt, daze, surprise

stunt   act, feat, exploit, performance, accomplishment

stupid   foolish, silly, dull, dumb, dim-witted, dense, *smart*

sturdy   strong, rugged, hardy, robust, vigorous, solid, durable, firm

stunt

stutter stammer, hesitate, falter

style mode, fashion, trend, vogue

stylish trendy, fashionable, chic, faddish, well-dressed, *drab*

subject issue, topic, matter, theme, point, question, text

substitute replace, rearrange, exchange, change, switch, swap

subtract take away, withdraw, remove, deduct, *add*

successful victorious, prosperous, accomplished, well-off, fortunate

sudden abrupt, unexpected, hasty

sufficient adequate, plenty, enough, *insufficient*

suffocate choke, stifle, smother

suggestion hint, plan, proposal, offer

suitable correct, appropriate, proper, fitting, *improper*

sum amount, quantity, total

summary digest, outline, review, accounting

summit top, peak, crown

sunny warm, bright, cheerful, pleasant, *dull*

sunrise sunup, daybreak, dawn, morning, *sunset*

sunset twilight, evening, dusk, sundown, nightfall, *sunrise*

sunny

superb admirable, splendid, glorious, fine, excellent, magnificent, grand, great, sensational, divine, wonderful, marvelous

superior   greater, higher, first-rate

supernatural   unearthly, mystical, ghostly

supervise   oversee, lead, direct, manage, run, control, guide, head, command, govern, boss

supply   furnish, give, provide

support   assist, aid, help, encourage, serve

suppose   presume, imagine, think, believe, consider

supreme   highest, utmost, paramount

sure   definite, positive, certain, *uncertain*

surplus   spare, additional, extra, excess, leftover, *shortage*

surprise   amaze, astound, astonish, stun, shock, startle

surrender   quit, yield, give up

surround   encircle, hem in, wrap

survive   last, remain, live

suspect   mistrust, question, doubt, distrust, *trust*

surprise

suspense   anxiety, uneasiness, uncertainty

suspension   1. dismissal, removal

suspension   2. pause, break, interruption, intermission

swab   mop, scrub, cleanse, wipe

swap   switch, exchange, trade, barter

swat   smack, whack, hit, strike

sway   reel, rock, swing, swagger

swear   1. pledge, vow, promise, guarantee

swear   2. curse, denounce

sweep   brush, clean, vacuum

sweep

sweet

sweet 1. pleasant, lovely, charming, adorable, agreeable, *disagreeable*

sweet 2. sugary, syrupy, saccharine, *bitter*

swift fleet, fast, speedy, hasty, rapid, quick, *slow*

swindle hoax, cheat, bamboozle, defraud, trick

swing rock, sway, dangle, hang, reel

switch exchange, change, substitute, replace, swap, trade

sword blade, knife

symbol emblem, token

sympathy pity, understanding, empathy, compassion

symptom indication, mark, sign, clue

system manner, means, plan, method, habit, custom, procedure, style, way, arrangement

T

tag

tack add, affix, attach, join, fasten, clasp

tactful diplomatic, considerate, sensitive, kind, thoughtful, gracious, *tactless*

tag 1. trail, shadow, follow, tail, pursue

tag 2. name, label, brand

tail 1. pursue, shadow, follow, trail

tail   2. rear, back, end

take   1. get, capture, seize, obtain, receive, *give*

take   2. transport, convey, bring, carry

tale   account, story, myth, legend

talent   capability, ability, gift, know-how, forte, skill

talk   converse, discuss, speak, chat

tall   high, towering, lofty, *short*

tame   obedient, gentle, domesticated, mild, *wild*

tangle   snarl, knot, twist, snag

tantrum   flare-up, outburst, fit, scene, rage, fury,
   frenzy

tap   1. pat, rap

tap   2. spigot, faucet

tape   1. bind, wrap, fasten, tie

tape   2. recording

target   purpose, goal, aim, end, object

tart   tangy, sharp, bitter, sour, pungent, *sweet*

task   work, chore, job, duty, assignment, requirement

taste   savor, test, sample, sense

tavern   saloon, inn, pub, bar, cabaret

tax   tariff, toll, duty, charge

taxi   cab, hack

teach   educate, show, instruct, enlighten, inform,
   lead, tell, advise, tutor

team   crew, band, gang, group

tear   slit, cut, split, rip, slice, slash, sever

team

141

tease

tease   pester, bother, annoy, provoke, badger, nag

technique   system, method, procedure

televise   broadcast, telecast

tell   state, announce, report, relate, recite, inform, explain, communicate, convey

temper   disposition, condition, nature, character, mood

temperamental   emotional, unstable, moody, sensitive, touchy

temporary   short-lived, momentary, passing, transient, unstable, fleeting, *permanent*

tempt   lure, entice, attract, appeal, entrance, seduce

tend   care for, attend, administer, foster, nurse

tense   edgy, irritable, nervous, jumpy, anxious, strained, uptight, rigid, *relaxed*

term   time, period, duration

terrible   awful, horrible, dreadful, horrid, atrocious, vile, abominable, detestable, despicable, *wonderful*

terrific   glorious, wonderful, marvelous, splendid, magnificent, great, sensational, fabulous, *ordinary*

terrify   alarm, scare, frighten, petrify, shock, horrify, unnerve

territory   neighborhood, area, region, section, district, zone

test   1. quiz, question, examine, investigate, interrogate

test   2. sample, try, taste, experiment, attempt

text subject, issue, point, topic, theme, problem, thesis, copy

thankful appreciative, obliged, grateful

thaw defrost, melt

theater hall, playhouse, auditorium

thick massive, bulky, solid, broad, coarse, *thin*

thief crook, burglar, robber, housebreaker

thin slim, lean, skinny, slight, frail, slender, gaunt, *fat*

theater

think 1. presume, believe, judge, imagine, suppose, guess, expect, assume, suspect

think 2. reason, theorize, reflect, consider, muse, ponder, cogitate

thirsty dry, dehydrated, parched

thorough all-out, complete, intensive, entire, *incomplete*

thought 1. concept, notion, idea, reflection

thought 2. attention, care, concern, regard

thoughtful kind, considerate, tactful, sensitive, careful, *thoughtless*

thoughtless tactless, inconsiderate, insensitive, careless, unkind, *thoughtful*

threaten intimidate, bully, warn, terrorize, bulldoze, menace, harass, admonish

thrifty frugal, careful, economical, prudent, *wasteful*

thrilling enchanting, delightful, exciting, entrancing, stirring, inspiring, moving, breathtaking, *boring*

thrilling

143

throw fling, toss, pitch, heave, cast, hurl, chuck

thump strike, blow, pound, beat, knock, hit, jab, poke, punch

thunder bellow, clamor, crash

ticket 1. voucher, pass, token, credential

ticket 2. subpoena, summons, citation

tidy well-kept, orderly, neat, shipshape, trim, *sloppy*

tie bind, fasten, secure, wrap, strap, *untie*

tight firm, snug, rigid, taut, tense, *loose*

tilt lean, slant, slope, incline

timid bashful, reserved, shy, meek, modest, *bold*

tint dye, shade, color, stain

tiny minute, small, little, miniature, puny, *huge*

tip 1. point, end, extremity

tip 2. bonus, gratuity

tip 3. information, advice, suggestion, clue, pointer

tired fatigued, weary, exhausted, sleepy, drowsy, *rested*

tool

title heading, name, headline, caption

toll fee, fare, charge, tax

tone key, pitch, sound, intonation, note

tongue language, speech, talk

tool device, instrument, utensil, implement, apparatus, gadget

topple

top peak, apex, head, tip, crown, summit, *bottom*

topic theme, issue, subject, point, question, matter

topple drop, fall, collapse, tumble, overturn, sprawl

144

torch   flare, lantern, light

tornado   hurricane, tempest, windstorm

torture   torment, agony, pain, persecution

toss   fling, pitch, throw, sling, cast, hurl, heave

total   1. complete, entire, whole, *partial*

total   2. sum up, add, count

toss

touch   handle, feel, contact

tough   1. strong, hardy, durable, rugged, sturdy, robust, *weak*

tough   2. difficult, hard, obscure, complicated, rough, *easy*

tour   journey, trip, excursion, voyage

tournament   match, game, contest, sport, competition, play

tow   haul, pull, tug, drag, draw

tower   obelisk, monument, edifice

toxic   malignant, deadly, poisonous, venomous

trace   duplicate, outline, reproduce, copy, draw, sketch

track   course, path, road, trail

trade   1. switch, barter, exchange, bargain, swap, deal

trade   2. work, business, occupation, employment, line, craft

tradition   habit, custom, usage

tragic   disastrous, sad, catastrophic, calamitous, unfortunate, dreadful

trail 1. tail, chase, follow, pursue, track, shadow

trail 2. course, track, road, path

train 1. drill, teach, exercise, practice, condition, prepare, direct, groom

train 2. railroad cars

traitor informer, spy, betrayer, tattler

tramp vagabond, hobo, vagrant

transfer deliver, hand over, change, pass, sign over

transform change, convert, alter, shift

translate interpret

trap apprehend, snare, seize, catch, capture, hook, *release*

trash garbage, litter, scrap, waste, rubbish, junk, refuse

travel tour, journey, voyage

treasure 1. cherish, idolize, adore, value, appreciate, protect

treasure 2. riches, wealth, fortune

treat 1. handle, deal with, care for, tend to, regard

treat 2. thrill, pleasure, delight

treaty agreement, pact, alliance, understanding, commitment

tremble quiver, shudder, shake, quake

tremendous huge, colossal, gigantic, enormous, vast, giant, monumental, immense, *tiny*

trial 1. experiment, test, tryout

trial 2. hearing, inquest

treasure

tribe   clan, group, sect
tribute   compliment, praise, glorification, eulogy
trick   dupe, defraud, hoax, fool, deceive, mislead
trim   1. reduce, pare, cut, shave, lower
trim   2. adorn, decorate, ornament, beautify
trip   1. tumble, stagger, stumble, slip, falter, fall
trip   2. journey, voyage, expedition, excursion, tour
triumph   conquer, overcome, win
troop   squad, unit, company, group, team
trophy   prize, medal, award, honor, reward
trouble   difficulty, bother, disturbance, inconvenience
truant   shirker, absentee
truce   peace, cease-fire, armistice, lull
true   real, genuine, actual, authentic, pure, proper,
   right, valid, exact, accurate, correct, *false*
trust   rely, believe, accept, *mistrust, distrust*
try   sample, test, attempt, experiment, effort
tuck   fold, bend, crease, gather
tug   drag, tow, pull, draw, haul, yank
tumble   topple, fall, plunge, drop
tune   song, melody, music
tunnel   burrow, passage, canal, channel
turn   twirl, spin, swirl, rotate, twist, pivot
tutor   instruct, teach, educate, coach
twinkle   gleam, glimmer, sparkle, shine, glisten,
   glitter, blink
twirl   swirl, twist, turn, whirl

trick

trophy

twist

twist twirl, turn, swirl, spin
twitch writhe, jerk, shudder, shake, fidget
type sort, kind, species, variety, category, class, group, character
typical ordinary, usual, common, model, representative, characteristic
tyrant dictator, oppressor, ruler, slave driver, taskmaster, despot

U

ugly gruesome, hideous, unattractive, homely, repellent, *beautiful*
umpire judge, mediator, referee
unable incapable, unfit, powerless, incapacitated, *able*
unanimous harmonious, in accord, agreed, of one mind
unaware unknowing, ignorant, unmindful, unconscious
unbelievable 1. incredible, fantastic, absurd
unbelievable 2. doubtful, suspicious, questionable, *believable*

148

unbiased   fair, impartial, balanced, neutral

uncertain   unsure, doubtful, unpredictable,
undecided, speculative, insecure, *certain*

unchanged   constant, steady, same, unmoving,
changed, *different*

uncivilized   wild, primitive, prehistoric, savage,
unrefined, *civilized*

unclean   dirty, filthy, soiled, polluted

uncomfortable   unpleasant, cramped, awkward,
irritated, *comfortable*

uncommon   extraordinary, rare, unusual, odd,
unlikely, different, unique, original, novel, *common*

uncomfortable

unconscious   ignorant, unaware, senseless, out cold,
comatose, *conscious*

unconstitutional   illegal, unlawful, *legal*

uncover   show, disclose, expose, reveal, display,
conceal

undecided   unsure, vague, uncertain, doubtful,
indefinite, pending, undetermined, *decided*

under   beneath, below, *over*, *above*

underground   subterranean

underneath   below, beneath, under

understand   know, see, follow, comprehend, grasp,
appreciate, gather

undo   unfasten, untie, open

undress   strip, disrobe, unclothe, denude, *dress*

unemployed   jobless, unoccupied, idle, *employed*

underground

149

uneven

unequal uneven, mismatched, one-sided, irregular, *equal*

uneven unequal, irregular, lumpy

unexpected unforeseen, abrupt, sudden, accidental, unplanned, unanticipated, *expected*

unfair unjust, unreasonable, biased, *fair*

unfaithful disloyal, untrue, fickle, false, *faithful*

unfamiliar unusual, strange, different, new, odd, *familiar*

unfasten open, undo, unbutton, untie, loosen, *fasten, close*

unfold reveal, disclose, show, open, uncover, unmask

unfortunate unlucky, unhappy, ill-fated, sad, *fortunate, lucky*

unfriendly hostile, antisocial, aloof, distant, cool, withdrawn, *friendly*

unfriendly

ungrateful thankless, unappreciative, *grateful*

unhappy depressed, sad, gloomy, downhearted, grieving, sorrowful, blue, forlorn, glum, melancholy, *happy*

unhealthy ailing, sick, invalid, frail, weak, *healthy*

uniform costume, outfit

unify combine, blend, knit, merge, unite, *separate*

unimportant trivial, petty, unnecessary, minor, insignificant, *important*

union harmony, accord, unity

unique sole, singular, unequaled, one-of-a-kind

unit   measure, section, segment, part, portion

unite   join, link, collect, gather, assemble, fuse

unity   oneness, consolidation, solidarity

universe   world, galaxy, space

unkind   mean, nasty, cruel, rude, thoughtless, careless, ruthless, *kind*

unknown   mysterious, inscrutable, puzzling, unexplored, *known*

unlock   open, undo, unbolt, unfasten, discover, probe, penetrate, *lock*

unlucky   unfortunate, unhappy, ill-fated, doomed, misguided, *lucky*

unlucky

unnatural   abnormal, weird, unnerving, otherworldly, *natural*

unnecessary   needless, inessential, uncalled-for, useless, *necessary*

unoccupied   vacant, open, empty, available, *occupied*, *inhabited*

unpack   empty, unload, dump, *pack*

unpleasant   disagreeable, nasty, obnoxious, unlikable, offensive, disgusting, *pleasant*

unpopular   disliked, unloved, unappreciated, unwanted, *popular*

unprepared   unready, untrained, unwary, *prepared*, *ready*

unreal   imaginary, make-believe, false, *real*

unreasonable irrational, absurd, ridiculous, extreme, excessive, outrageous, *reasonable, rational*

unrest rebellion, disturbance, turmoil

unruly rowdy, wild, disorderly, disobedient, *orderly*

unsafe risky, dangerous, hazardous, perilous, *safe*

unsatisfactory second-rate, inferior, poor, inadequate, insufficient, *satisfactory*

unselfish generous, giving, kind, *selfish*

unsuccessful failing, incapable, disastrous, unfortunate, *successful*

unsure uncertain, stumbling, awkward, hesitant, self-conscious, *confident, sure*

untie

untie unfasten, undo, loosen, unclip, *tie*

untrained unskilled, unprepared, amateurish, *trained, skilled*

unusual extraordinary, different, rare, novel, original, uncommon, *usual*

unwilling resistant, reluctant, opposed, *willing*

unwise foolish, silly, senseless, foolhardy, *wise*

uphold maintain, support, back, defend

upright 1. erect, standing, vertical

upright 2. respectable, honorable, moral

uprising revolt, revolution, rebellion, riot

uproar clamor, racket, noise, tumult, disturbance, commotion, hubbub, *peace*

unusual

upset bother, unnerve, disturb, annoy, *soothe*

urge advise, prod, push, press, prompt, coax, *discourage*

urgent important, necessary, vital, essential, central, crucial, *unimportant*

use employ, utilize, handle, practice

useful handy, practical, helpful, beneficial, valuable, assisting, *useless*

useless trivial, valueless, worthless, meaningless, *useful*

usher escort, guide, show

usual everyday, ordinary, regular, common, normal, familiar, typical, *unusual*

V

vacant empty, uninhabited, available, open, unoccupied, *occupied*

vacation recess, break, leave, holiday

vacuum emptiness, vacancy, void

vague cloudy, blurry, indistinct, imprecise, inexact, unclear, *clear*, *precise*

vain egotistical, self-centered, proud, arrogant, haughty, smug, *modest*

vacant

vanish

valid   sound, true, logical, legal

valuable   precious, significant, important, costly, expensive

value   cost, worth, price

vandalism   defacement, ruination, destruction

vanish   disappear, fade, evaporate, *appear*

vapor   gas, steam, mist, fog

variety   mixture, assortment, diversity

various   many, different, several, assorted, numerous

vary   alter, change, switch, shift

vast   enormous, expansive, huge, immense, great, *tiny*

vegetable   plant, flora, fruit, growth, legume

vegetation   plants, growth, undergrowth, underbrush, flora

vehicle   car, conveyance, bus, carrier, carriage

veil   cover, mask, screen, disguise, *unveil, uncover*

venom   poison, spite, bitterness, ill will

verdict   ruling, decision, judgment, finding, opinion

verge   edge, border, brink, rim

verse   1. rhyme, poetry

verse   2. section, passage, division, part

version   description, story, opinion, account, interpretation

vertical   upright, erect, up-and-down, *horizontal*

veto   disallow, deny, refuse, *approve*

vibrate   quiver, shake

vice   fault, failing, sin, crime, *virtue*

vicious

vicious   savage, fierce, ferocious, ruthless, cruel, brutal, mean, wicked, evil

victim   sufferer, underdog, loser, prey, dupe

victory   winning, success, triumph, overcoming, *defeat*

view   scene, sight, picture, vista, panorama

village   town, hamlet, community

villain   rascal, scoundrel, knave, devil, bad guy

violate   disobey, break, rupture

violence   frenzy, anger, rage, fury, force, intensity

virtue   goodness, purity, innocence, merit, worth, *vice*

vision   1. perception, eyesight

vision   2. illusion, image, mirage, fantasy, dream, idea

visitor   guest, company, caller

vital   lively, alive, vivacious, alert, active

vivid   bright, clear, strong

vocal   spoken, voiced, uttered, oral

voice   express, utter, verbalize, say, articulate, tell

void   emptiness, vacuum, nothingness

volunteer   enlist, offer, come forward

vote   ballot, election, choice, selection

vow   oath, promise, pledge, agreement

voyage   cruise, journey, excursion, crossing, expedition

vulgar   coarse, common, crude, crass

villain

W

wag

weak

wad   lump, mass, hunk, chunk

wag   flop, flap, wave, shake, swing

wages   payment, salary, earnings

wake   arouse, get up, arise

walk   saunter, amble, stroll, strut

wallet   billfold, purse, pocketbook, moneybag

wallop   slap, belt, smack, crack, strike, hit, slug, beat, whack

wander   meander, drift, stray, ramble, rove, roam

want   long for, wish for, desire, crave, need

war   feud, fight, battle, conflict, combat, struggle

warehouse   storehouse, depot, supply, dump

warm   heat, inflame

warn   alert, inform, notify, caution, foretell, intimidate, threaten, admonish

wary   watchful, alert, careful, guarded, suspicious

wash   scrub, clean, launder, wipe

waste   misuse, squander, misspend, *save*

watch   1. see, observe, look at

watch   2. defend, protect, guard, police, shield

watchful   observant, mindful, careful, alert

wave   flap, move, sway, flop

wax   shine, polish, glaze

weak   frail, feeble, powerless, incapable, *strong*

wealthy

wealthy well-off, rich, well-to-do, comfortable, prosperous, affluent, *poor*

weapon firearm, sword, gun, munition

wear 1. dress, have on, don

wear 2. deteriorate, decay, corrode

weary tired, fatigued, worn out, exhausted

weather climate, temperature, conditions, environment

wed marry, unite, join

wedge jam, squeeze, push between

weight girth, poundage, heft, burden, importance, seriousness

weird strange, peculiar, odd, queer, spooky, creepy, unusual, eerie, bizarre, abnormal, *normal*

welcome greet, hail, encourage, receive

whack smack, slug, wallop, belt, beat, strike, hit, thrash, crack

whip thrash, flog, beat, strike, crack

whisper murmur, mutter, hiss, mumble

whistle pipe, flute

whole entire, total, complete, full, *partial*

wicked bad, sinful, evil, demonic, cruel, mean, vile, vicious, *good*

wide roomy, expansive, broad, large, *narrow*

wife spouse, married woman, mate

wig hair piece, toupee

wild

wild   1. uncivilized, untamed, primitive, savage, ferocious, natural, *tame, civilized*

wild   2. rowdy, boisterous, reckless, crazy, frenzied, *calm*

willing   open, agreeable, consenting, ready, *unwilling*

win   triumph, succeed, prevail, overcome, *lose*

1. wind   gust, breeze, air, draft, current

2. wind   coil, twist, turn, wrap

wire   cable, telegraph

wise   knowing, knowledgeable, smart, clever, scholarly, educated, learned

wish   want, long for, desire, yearn, crave

withdraw   pull back, retreat, subtract, deduct, remove, *advance, deposit*

without   needing, wanting, lacking, less, minus, missing, deficient in, *with*

witty   amusing, clever, humorous, funny, comic

wonderful   fabulous, great, glorious, divine, marvelous, grand, sensational, superb, splendid

woods   forest, timberland

work   1. toil, labor, effort

work   2. run, manage, operate, handle

workout   exercise, training, drill, practice

world   Earth, universe, sphere, globe

worn   secondhand, old, used, frayed, shabby, ragged, *new*

worried   disturbed, concerned, troubled, edgy, nervous, upset, *calm*

worship   cherish, idolize, adore, revere

worst   lowest, meanest, least good

worthless   useless, valueless, base, trivial

wound   hurt, injury, pain, bruise, scar

wrap   sheathe, envelop, cover, surround, encompass, bind

wreck   demolish, ruin, destroy

wring   wrench, twist, squeeze

wrinkle   crinkle, pleat, muss, crush

wrong   inaccurate, mistaken, faulty, incorrect, improper, *right*

worried

wrap

X

x-ray   photograph, picture

Y

yacht   boat, ship, sloop, cruiser
yank   pull, jerk, tug, twist
yard   court, pen, patio, lawn
yarn   1. thread, wool
yarn   2. tall tale, story, fib
yell   cry, scream, shout, howl, yelp, call, screech, shriek, bawl
yelp   bark, howl, squawk
yield   1. bear, provide, give, produce, bring forth, supply
yield   2. give in, give up, surrender, sacrifice, resign
yoke   harness, chain, tie, bond, union
young   juvenile, youthful, childish, *old*
youngster   youth, minor, child, kid, adolescent

Z

zero

zero   none, nil, nothing
zest   enthusiasm, gusto, relish, tang
zone   neighborhood, section, district, region, ward, territory, area
zoo   menagerie
zoom   whiz, zip, speed, fly

160